Ghost Towns and Drowned Towns of West Kootenay

ELSIE G. TURNBULL

The ghostly remains of the Arlington Hotel in Slocan City in the 1950s.

CONTENTS

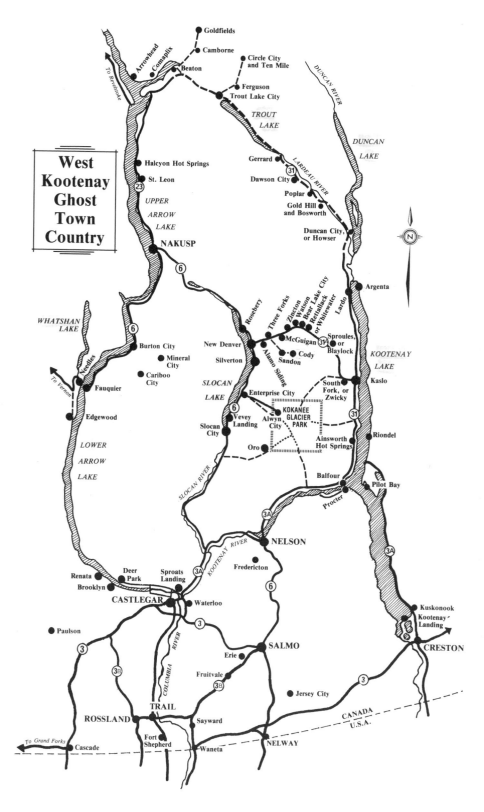

West Kootenay Ghost Town Country

FRONT COVER
The remaining abandoned buildings of Sandon wait to be crushed by winter snow or swept away by Carpenter Creek. (See page 72.)

BACK COVER
Once Silverton's wharf bustled as mountain mines yielded their silver treasure. Today it waits to collapse into Slocan Lake. (See page 83.)
Bottom: Zincton in the 1960s. The mountains of West Kootenay once throbbed with similar mining communities which have been reclaimed by the forest. Of Zincton, nothing remains. (See page 67.)

PHOTO CREDITS
B.C. Provincial Archives: 8-9, 13, 17, 19, 22, 23, 25, 33, 38, 40, 45, 49, 54, 59, 61, 64-65, 66, 68, 69, 70, 72, 73, 76-77, 80-81, 84, 89, 92, 95, 96-97, 99, 101, 103, 107; Glenbow-Alberta Institute: 56-57; Heritage House: 90; Public Archives of Canada: 33; Silverton Historical Society: 86; Tourism B.C.: 12-13, 76; Vancouver Public Library: 32, 47, 49, 51, 52-53, 95, 103, 109; F.H. Buckley: 23; Donovan Clemson: 76, 99, 107; Mrs. H. Lakes: 43; E. Turnbull: 67, 70.

CANADIAN CATALOGUING IN PUBLICATION DATA

Turnbull, Elsie G. (Elsie Grant), 1903-
    Ghost Towns and Drowned Towns of West Kootenay

ISBN 0-919214-61-4

1. Cities and towns, Ruined, extinct, etc. - British Columbia - Kootenay Region. 2. Kootenay Region (B.C.) - History. 3. Kootenay Region (B.C.) - Description and travel. I. Title.
FC3845.K7T87 1988   971.1'45   C88-091023-2
F1089.K7T87 1988

HERITAGE HOUSE PUBLISHING COMPANY LTD.
Unit #8 17921 55 Ave., Surrey, B.C. V3S 6C4

Printed in Canada

PRINTING HISTORY
First Edition — 1988
Second Printing — 1990
Third Printing — 1994

The Kootenays

In general, this region of southeastern B.C. extends from the Rocky Mountains some 280 miles (450 km) westward to the Monashee, and from the U.S. border northward to the general area of the Trans-Canada Highway. With the Selkirk and Purcell Mountains in its center it is a great inland island of forest, ice and snow, often called "The Switzerland of North America," although it is twice as large as Switzerland. Its topography consists of a series of north-south mountain ranges separated by deep valleys and large rivers and lakes, including Kootenay which is over 70 miles (112 km) long, B.C.'s third largest natural lake. The Kootenays embrace nearly all of the watersheds of the Columbia and Kootenay Rivers and are unofficially separated into two regions, West and East Kootenay.

West Kootenay extends from the Purcell Mountains west to the Arrow Lakes and from the U.S. border northward to the Lardeau. It is larger than the East Kootenay which extends from the Rocky Mountains westward to the Purcell Mountains and northward from the U.S. border to the Golden area.

The East Kootenay is the headwaters of both the Kootenay and Columbia Rivers which break free of the Rocky Mountains only a few miles apart. The Columbia River, on its 1,300-mile (2,100-km) journey to the Pacific Ocean flows northwestward past Golden to make its "Big Bend" around the Selkirk Mountains before angling southward to create the Arrow Lakes in West Kootenay and join the Pacific Ocean at the Washington-Oregon border.

The Kootenay River, by contrast, heads southward into Montana. Here

In the early 1880s, prospectors rowed boats or paddled canoes and rafts up Kootenay Lake where they discovered massive mineral outcroppings. For over 50 years the lake was the main transportation link for scores of settlers and communities.

it becomes the Kootenai and loops northwestward, cutting off a corner of Idaho before sweeping back into B.C. where it again becomes the Kootenay. It creates Kootenay Lake, then flows southwestward 22 miles (35 km) to join the Columbia River opposite Castlegar.

The first white man to explore the region was David Thompson of the North West Company, a fur-trading rival of the Hudson's Bay Company. He was not only Canada's greatest geographer-explorer but also the foremost in North America. Beginning in 1807 Thompson spent 22 years in the West, travelling some 50,000 miles (80,000 km) by canoe and horseback in summer, snowshoes and dog team in winter. He established a successful fur trade west of the Rocky Mountains and mapped most of the Columbia River watershed, in the process becoming the first man to follow the river from its Rocky Mountain headwaters to the Pacific Ocean. His exploration covered much of the territory which is now Montana, Idaho and Washington and he took possession of it all for England. British statesmen, however, attached little value to the region and in the 1840s it became part of the United States.

Because of the West Kootenay's rugged topography, there were few Indians and no trading posts until 1856 when Fort Shepherd was built on the Columbia River near the border. Not until the early 1880s did the West Kootenay become generally known, the stimulus not furs but minerals. The Selkirks and Purcells yielded base metals in lavish quantity — the lead and zinc of the Blue Bell, copper of the Silver King, lead-zinc-gold of Ymir and Sheep Creek Mines. Out of the Slocan poured a stream of silver-lead-zinc ore, matched only in value by the gold-copper of Rossland Camp. It was the latter which led to erection of a smelter at Trail Creek Landing (today's Trail) on the Columbia River.

Much of the capital for early mine development came from the United States and ore shipments were made by boat to American railroads and American smelters. Soon, however, British and Eastern Canada capital poured into the region and the Canadian Pacific Railway entered competition for trade. By the mid-1880s the C.P.R. had completed its main line through the Rockies to Golden and Revelstoke and was ready to challenge the Northern Pacific that spanned Idaho and Washington, as well as the Great Northern which constructed feeder lines toward mines along the Columbia and Kootenay waterways and then installed a fleet of steamboats and barges on lake and river. Acquisition by the Great Northern of the Spokane Falls & Northern Railway, and its extension into Rossland as the Red Mountain Railway, led to the building in 1893 of the U.S. Nelson & Fort Sheppard which connected at Troup Junction with vessels on Kootenay Lake. Then the Great Northern entered the Slocan area with the Kaslo & Slocan Railway. Meanwhile, the C.P.R. laid track between Kootenay and Arrow Lakes and put a fleet of sternwheelers on the Arrow Lakes that connected with a branch line at Arrowhead running down from the main line at Revelstoke. Access to the Slocan was provided by the Nakusp and Slocan Railway from Nakusp to Sandon.

In 1898, under charter of the B.C. Southern Railway, the C.P.R. began laying track for a southern line through the Crowsnest Pass to the Kootenays, meeting the challenge of the Great Northern from its Bedlington

& Nelson at Kuskonook and Kootenay Landing. The latter also planned going up the east side of the lake to Argenta and Duncan City.

Both Canadians and Americans put vessels on the Arrow and Kootenay Lakes while the C.P.R. also offered steamboat service on Slocan and Trout Lakes. As time went on American competition disappeared and the C.P.R. extended its control. Its fleet of sternwheelers plied the waterways for over 60 years, transporting ore from all the mines, as well as fruit and produce from orchard and farm, until the automobile took over.

Today the railways have been largely replaced by paved highways which provide access to all of the West Kootenay. Included are Highway 3, the main link from the Coast Mountains at Hope through the Rockies into Alberta; Highway 3B through Rossland and Trail; Highway 3A from Castlegar through Nelson to Balfour, across Kootenay Lake by ferry then southeastward to Creston; Highway 6 from Salmo then via Nelson and Slocan to the Okanagan; Highway 31 from Balfour northward through Kaslo to the Lardeau; and Highway 31A from Kaslo to New Denver.

A major change in West Kootenay's transportation pattern and many communities occurred in 1965 when construction began on the $500 million Columbia River power and flood control project. Under this co-operative Canadian-U.S. venture Canada agreed to build three dams — two on the Columbia River and one on the Duncan at the north end of Kootenay Lake.

One of the Columbia dams is at Mica 85 miles (136 km) north of Revelstoke. This massive structure rises some 650 feet (195 m) above the river bed and is over one-half mile (1 km) wide. The world's largest earth-filled dam, it created an inland sea 135 miles (216 km) long.

The other Columbia dam is the Hugh Keenleyside at Castlegar. It is 170 ft. (52 m) high with a lock to permit small craft to utilize Arrow Lake. It backed up the Columbia River to Revelstoke, flooding the 20 miles (32 km) of river channel between Lower and Upper Arrow Lakes. The dam created a lake some 155 miles (250 km) long and destroyed farms, summer homes and communities. Later, B.C. Hydro built another massive 500-ft. (150-m) dam 3 miles (5 km) north of Revelstoke. It backed water upstream almost to the Mica Dam.

In addition to the drowned communities in West Kootenay there are dozens of vanished ones hidden in the valleys and mountains. Many throbbed with life, while others existed only in glowing newspaper advertisements or in the fertile imaginations of mining and townsite promoters.

As T.G. Blackstone noted in the *Trail Creek News* on August 26, 1898, after he had bought the Centre Star Mine near Rossland:

"This may be extravagant anticipation but the sober truth seems to be that towns and cities will grow up in the mountains and tens of thousands of men will be employed within a few years where but yesterday the mountain goat and the brown bear were in undisputed possession."

While history has proved his "extravagant anticipation" to be somewhat optimistic, towns and cities did grow up in the mountains. Trail, Rossland, Castlegar, Nelson, Kaslo and others trace their heritage to the early 1880s when prospectors canoed and rafted up Kootenay Lake. Unknowingly, they laid the foundation for the West Kootenay of today — live towns as well as ghost towns.

Chapter One

SOUTHERN KOOTENAY LAKE

Ainsworth Hot Springs

Dating to 1883, Ainsworth has the distinction of being the first community on Kootenay Lake and for several years the largest. Its story began in 1882 when a prospecting party of three U.S. residents, which included George J. Ainsworth, paddled up Kootenay Lake. On the west shore of the lake where hot water bubbled from the rocks they staked 160 acres for a townsite and the minerals underneath. A community which developed was called Hot Springs Camp, but changed when Ainsworth received official title and named it after his family, a name even then well-known to B.C. During the 1858 gold rush to the Fraser River, George's father, John C. Ainsworth, arrived from Oregon with a sternwheeler, the *Umatilla*. It became the first vessel to navigate Harrison Lake and the Fraser River to Yale.

Following the successful 1882 prospecting trip by George Ainsworth, Kootenay Lake attracted prospectors by the score. The next year the mountains bordering the huge inland sea were being explored from lakeshore to timberline and above. The prospectors' search was formidable since the area was total wilderness, harsh and unforgiving.

The first man to explore the area was North America's great geographer, David Thompson. In 1808 he described it as "...stupendous

and solitary Wilds covered with eternal Snow'' where ''Mountain [is] connected to Mountain to immense Glaciers, the collection of Ages.'' When the snow and glaciers melted in the spring winds and summer sun the effect ''. . . equalled the Thunder in Sound, overturning everything less than solid Rock in its Course, sweeping the Mountain Forests, whole acres at a time from the very Roots, leaving not a Vestige behind.''

But like Thompson, prospectors were a breed who never flinched from the challenge of the wilderness. They built canoes and rafts from logs in the forest and paddled up the 73-mile- (117-km-) long lake. Among them

Two 1890s views of Ainsworth, the first community on Kootenay Lake. In the lower photo the white building near left center is the Olson Hotel, its famous two-storey outhouse at the rear.

were Henry Cody and 19-year-old Charles Olson. Cody discovered a series of caves that still bear his name while Olson, who paddled up the lake on a raft, staked the Highland Mine. It became the largest producer of lead in the British Empire and Olson one of Ainsworth's leading citizens.

Stimulated by rich strikes which led to the development of mines such as the Number One, Krao, and Little Donald, Ainsworth quickly became the largest community on Kootenay Lake. Facilities, though, tended to be basic as newspaperman Randall H. Kemp discovered when he passed through in 1889, equipped with "a roll of blankets and a valise." He later wrote that "for a bed I had a section of the floor of Fletcher & Co.'s log cabin store." Of various stopping places he noted: "Some set up good grub and some don't; some have beds with spring mattresses and some have beds without mattresses."

Another visitor was the Kootenay's legendary newspaperman Robert Thornton Lowery. In 1895 he observed that Ainsworth "... is the only place in Canada where a frog concert can be heard every evening of the year. This is owing to the hot springs that bubble up on the townsite. The frogs keep under the houses, where the hot water oozes from the earth, and sing their solos and duets without any regard to, or interruption from, the iciest weather that the district can produce."

A problem common to most pioneer communities was transportation since the only access was by water. There was an improvement in 1891 when the *Nelson* became the first sternwheeler on Kootenay Lake and in summer provided regular service. Unfortunately, she didn't operate in winter. Then supplies arrived by packhorse or over the ice on sleighs and prices rose by 300 per cent. Potatoes, for instance, jumped from $1 a 100 pounds to $3, the wages a miner earned for a 10-hour day.

To combat the supply problem, the community decided to build its own sternwheeler. On May 4, 1892, the *City of Ainsworth* was launched. When she returned from her maiden voyage she was welcomed with "three lusty cheers and a salute of dynamite."

By now the community was flourishing; the local paper, the *Hot Springs News*, reporting that "John L. Retallack, late owner of the Kaslo Slocan Railway, is firm in the belief that the future of Ainsworth is as bright as a new-minted 20-dollar piece."

The paper also noted that Ainsworth "... presents the liveliest appearance of any town on the lake." Since beer was 50 cents a gallon and whiskey $1 a quart the liveliness was understandable. It also offered over a dozen hotels with one of them, McKinnon House built in 1885, (a year before Vancouver was born) featuring water piped in from the hot springs

Best known hotelman was Charles Olson, the young boy who rafted up the lake in 1883. As Kootenay Lake historian Edna H. Hanic wrote in Heritage House book *Pioneer Days in British Columbia: Volume Four*:

"He started in the business when he was 21 and continued until he died in 1926. During those years he operated at various times the Hotel Hot Springs, the Ainsworth and the Olson. The Olson Hotel was a wooden building with a high false front. There were two entrances, their relative size indicating which part of the hotel was the most popular. A small door opened into a hall, the office and the stairway to the bedrooms; two large double doors led into the saloon. Upstairs a hallway ran down the center of the building with five bedrooms on each side. This hallway continued through the back door to a raised walkway which led to the hotel's most unusual feature — a two-storey outhouse.

"Here were two compartments, one for men and one for women, each containing a porcelain bowl covered with a wooden seat. The main floor had the same two conveniences, but a patron in the saloon had to go out a side door and down a path to reach them. To prevent the four luxurious fixtures from freezing in winter, Mrs. Olson heated them with coal-oil lamps. In very cold weather she wrapped the bowls in her husband's old raccoon coat and blankets.

"While Mrs. Olson was in charge of the dining room, Charles presided at the bar. He spared no expense, sending to France for brandy, Sweden for herring, and other countries for their specialities. He also purchased a solid mahogany baroque-style bar in Spokane Falls for $1,000, an enormous sum in the 1880s. It was backed by huge French bevelled mirrors in an ornate frame in front of which were shelves filled with sparkling glasses and liquor bottles.

"The cheerful 270-pound host was himself a drawing card, one of the many colorful characters on Kootenay Lake. His daily consumption of a quart of liquor was well known but it didn't seem to bother him. One day he won a bet in the bar by going out and lifting a horse. He took part in everything new — even making a special trip to Nelson to ride in that town's first automobile."

Unfortunately, Olson's hotel and twelve others were destroyed in a fire on April 6, 1896, which virtually wiped out Ainsworth. Rebuilding started immediately but the community was already in decline. Kaslo, some 12 miles (19 km) to the north, became the gateway to the rich Slocan mining region, cutting heavily into Ainsworth's trade. Then in November 1898 the *City of Ainsworth* was caught in a storm on Kootenay Lake and sank with the loss of nine lives.

Although no large mine ever came into development in Ainsworth, from 1889 to 1930 production was fairly steady. Then came a period of idleness but increased metal prices during and after World War Two revived interest in the camp. Yale Lead and Zinc Mines Limited built a nucleus around old claims first uncovered in the 1890s. A flotation mill was erected south of Ainsworth and operation continued until 1961.

Today scars of old mine workings are hidden by new growth, while houses and buildings at the Highland and other old claims have been flattened. Ainsworth lies unspoiled on a forested hillside. At its feet Kootenay Lake calls to fishermen and boating enthusiasts, and the hot springs have been developed.

A feature of the springs is a horseshoe-shaped cave which has been built up over the centuries with coats of different colored minerals. A hot shower of mineralized water falls from the roof into a pool, forming a natural steam bath. The healing waters, enjoyed first by the Indians then the miners of the 1880s, are increasingly popular. Open all year, they ensure that West Kootenay's first community will not join several score of her sisters in oblivion.

Pilot Bay and Riondel

In the spring of 1882 a U.S. prospector named Robert Evan Sproule and two companions set out from Bonners Ferry, Idaho, in a rowboat for a prospecting trip up Kootenay Lake. Noting rusty stains on the face of a rock bluff on the eastern shore, they landed and staked the whole promontory, calling their claims the Blue Bell "after the small flower which covered the ground in profusion." That was the preliminary to tragic events which would involve claim jumping, murder and a hanging.

Sproule was not the only miner looking at Kootenay Lake that summer. Thomas B. Hammill was seeking minerals for his employers, Captain John Ainsworth and his son, George. The Ainsworths were railroad and steamboat men from Portland who were planning to build a rail line connecting Kootenay and Arrow Lakes. For them Hammill staked the Kootenay Chief, Comfort and Ruby claims next to Sproule's Blue Bell. Bad feelings soon arose between the two. Mining recorder William Fernie later stated that "Hammill jumped Sproule's Blue Bell claim while Sproule jumped Hammill's Kootenay Chief, Comfort and Ruby." Legal redress was sought

and the judge divided the claims, awarding the Blue Bell to Sproule. The legal decision, unfortunately, wasn't the final solution.

Sproule now disposed of the Blue Bell to Dr. Wilbur A. Hendryx of Minneapolis who organized the Kootanie Mining and Smelting Company. As part payment, Sproule took shares in the Smelting Company but worked the claim under contract. Hammill reputedly acquired by purchase a part share in the Blue Bell, an action which caused Sproule to threaten his life if he set foot on the property.

During the morning of June 1, 1885, while Hammill was working on the Blue Bell claim a shot rang out. About noon Nick Belnouf, a workman on his way to lunch, discovered Hammill. He had been shot in the back. Although still alive, in his agony he had beaten his face bloody against the rocks. Hammill was carried to a shack but died soon after.

A miner then rowed across Kootenay Lake to Hot Springs Camp (the original name for Ainsworth Hot Springs) to get Provincial Police Constable Henry Anderson. After questioning the men, who appeared reluctant to talk, Anderson learned that Sproule that morning had asked one of the miners, Adam Wolfe, for his rifle and shells. At noon, when Wolfe returned to the bunkhouse, his rifle was there, a spent cartridge in the breech.

The Blue Bell Mine and Riondel. When the mine closed the community, unlike most in similar circumstances, didn't become a ghost town. Today it survives as a retirement center.

Below: The smelter at Pilot Bay with the sternwheeler *Spokane* at the dock. Only the ruins of the chimneys remain.

Sproule wasn't around but Anderson found a man who had seen him get into a rowboat carrying his own rifle.

The Constable and an Indian rowed after Sproule. Four days later they arrested him, Sproule protesting that he wasn't fleeing. He was on his way to the Kootanie Mining and Smelting Company's office across the border and had even fished as he rowed down the lake. Nevertheless, he was taken to Victoria where his trial opened in December 1885. It was to echo not only across Canada to England but also to the U.S. capital of Washington, D.C. Prosecuting Sproule was A.E. Davie who would become premier of B.C. the following year. Defending Sproule was Theodore Davie who also would become a B.C. premier.

On December 10, 1885, the jury brought in a verdict of guilty but with a recommendation for mercy. Sproule was sentenced to hang, execution date March 6, 1886. He was given a reprieve until April 6, then 24 hours before his meeting with the hangman, reprieved until May 6. By now, public opinion in Victoria was on Sproule's side, especially in view of the jury's recommendation for mercy. Three days before the May 6 execution date, came word from Ottawa of another reprieve — this time to June 4, followed by another postponement to July 6.

On June 20 Sproule learned that the Supreme Court of Canada had declared his trial void because the crime had been committed in the West Kootenay but the trial had taken place in Victoria. The Provincial Government, however, was determined to hang Sproule. It appealed the Supreme Court decision. Meanwhile, Sproule was given another reprieve — his fifth. The Supreme Court then ruled that the trial had been legal. Sproule was again sentenced to hang, this time on October 1, 1886. Defence counsel Davie desperately attempted to get another reprieve from the Minister of Justice at Ottawa but was refused. It was now only hours from the execution time, the scaffold, rope and coffin ready. Incredibly, on the afternoon before the execution, Sproule was again reprieved. He was now to hang on October 29, 1886.

The reason for this delay was that both the British and U.S. Governments had asked the Canadian Government to take another look at the case. As the editor of the *Victoria Colonist* wrote: "...it's a refinement of cruelty to hang him now."

Nevertheless, Ottawa permitted Sproule to be sentenced to death for the seventh time. The date was set for October 29. But there was one last hope.

So great was public opinion in Victoria in favor of Sproule that Mayor James Fell journeyed to Ottawa at his own expense to present a petition. It stressed that the jury had recommended mercy and that there was much doubt about Sproule's guilt. Mayor Fell even met with Prime Minister Sir John A. Macdonald. All was in vain. Sproule, protesting his innocence, was hanged.

"If he was guilty," an editorial in the *Colonist* stated, "then in deference to contrary opinion, he should have had commutation."

The *New York Tribune* was much more blunt. "The defendant was the victim of a foul conspiracy ... an innocent man had been murdered...."

A few days after Sproule was hanged, word came that he had inherited about $100,000 from an estate in Boston.

Meanwhile, the Kootanie Mining and Smelting Company had secured all the claims on the promontory and proceeded to operate the Blue Bell. Two small steamboats, *Surprise* and *Galena*, were put on the lake to carry ore to the railhead at Bonners Ferry in Idaho. Then in 1891 the Smelting Company decided to treat the ore locally by erecting a smelter. The site chosen was on Lighthouse Point, 8 miles (13 km) down the lake from the Blue Bell Mine. On the narrow neck of land between Kootenay Lake and Pilot Bay appeared a roasthouse, a mill building and a smelter.

Joshua Davies and J.A. Sayward built a sawmill, while a townsite was laid out with W.M. Newton as resident agent. The Galena Trading Company, managed by Hamilton Byers, sold drygoods and groceries. Dave Clark built a two-storey hotel with 13 rooms while an enterprising prospector provided accommodation of a different kind. He brought in some houseboats, anchored them and established a "floating" red-light district.

Smelting started in March 1895 and by the end of the year over 3,000 tons of silver-lead bullion had been shipped. Then difficulties arose. Flux used in the smelting process was hard to obtain, the ore had low silver and high lead content, and the cost of smelting coal was high. The Company decided to close the smelter until completion of the B.C. Southern Railway in 1898 reduced the price of coal. During 1897 the mill was reactivated but by 1899 the assets of the Kootanie Mining and Smelting Company were taken over by the Bank of Montreal. Fortune would later smile on the Blue Bell Mine but not the smelter town of Pilot Bay. The first closure of the smelter had reduced the population to 150, but the sawmill remained in operation. Then in 1902 it shut down and most of the families left. The one-room school which had functioned for five years closed and the town of Pilot Bay disappeared. Today broken bricks, cellar foundations and two brick stacks that are a curiosity to those travelling by car ferry across Kootenay Lake are all that remain.

There is, however, a tangible legacy of the Blue Bell saga. In 1905 the properties were purchased by a French syndicate with Count Edouard Riondel at its head. The syndicate formed the Canadian Metal Company to operate the mine and appointed S.S. Fowler manager. By 1921, 70 residents lived in a hamlet called Riondel but its future appeared uncertain since that year the French company withdrew. The Blue Bell then lay idle until 1924 when it was acquired by S.S. Fowler and B.L. Eastman.

They formed the New Metal Company but in 1931 sold the property to the gigantic Consolidated Mining & Smelting Company of Trail. Bad luck, however, still haunted the area. The 1930s depression followed by World War Two delayed development, but in 1951 the Blue Bell started a yearly output of 250,000 tons of lead-zinc ore. Riondel became a bustling community of 600 people, its future seemingly assured by a rich mine backed by one of the world's largest smelter complexes. But prosperity was fleeting. In 1971 the ore was exhausted and the mine closed. Many working residents moved away but Cominco sold land and houses to retirees and Riondel remains very much alive as a town, with golf course, swimming beach and fishing in Kootenay Lake.

Fredericton

A common denominator of several West Kootenay communities is that they were born as the result of the accidental discovery of a rich outcropping of ore. One such discovery has as its legacy today's city of Nelson, for many years known as the Queen City of the Kootenays and still a major business and administrative center.

The story began in the fall of 1886 when a group of ranchers from Colville, Washington, set off on a prospecting trip to Canada. Included were Winslow and Osner Hall, their six sons, three cousins and two friends. With 21 pack animals they threaded up the Columbia River to Beaver Creek which they followed to the Salmo Valley, then ascended a peak overlooking Kootenay Lake. They found nothing of interest. Nothing, that is, until Willie White and Tommy Hall went looking for their horses, or was it grouse, or marmots?

Many versions of the tale exist but at any rate the boys paused for a smoke. Willie White picked up a "funny bright kind of rock" whose green and blue colors were recognized by older members of the group as peacock copper. Clearing away earth and underbrush they found a large outcrop. Because of the lateness of the season the men could not stay to examine it but were forced to leave. Back in Colville assay runs disclosed ore high in metals so the group waited impatiently for spring in order to return to their bonanza. They would not be alone. Other prospectors followed them to the slopes of the unnamed peak and soon christened it Toad Mountain. Several versions of this story also have been told but John Houston, editor of the *Nelson Tribune* and the city's first mayor, ascribed its naming to two prospectors who were filling out a form for recording. As they were about to describe the unnamed mountain one prospector saw a toad hop out from beneath a log and said: "Let's call the blame thing Toad Mountain!"

The claims which the Hall group staked proved very rich and became the Silver King Mine. The original locators worked it for awhile but then sold to an English syndicate which became the Hall Mining & Smelting Company. A smelter was built on the lakeshore at the foot of the mountain and ore brought down the steep hillside by aerial tram. A community which appeared on the lakeshore was named Salisbury, then Nelson, while at the minehead a town known as Fredericton housed miners and their families.

Lying 4,000 ft. (1,220 m) above Kootenay Lake, Fredericton was a tiny gash in the thick balsam and spruce forest, 9 miles (14.4 km) by winding road from Nelson. A dozen or so houses had been built on the sidehill, the rear at ground level but the front supported by 12-ft. (3.6-m) cribbing. Plain and unpainted, they were divided into four-room apartments with a leanto at the back for woodpile and supplies. One small pantry under the stairs replaced cupboards and closets, while a large kitchen range and a heater in the living room provided heat. There was no plumbing. Water had to be carried from a mine building up the hill, while a dim bulb dangling from the ceiling provided light.

A small store carried supplies, although most of the residents did their shopping from Eaton's catalogue. Between the two mine portals were office buildings, a sawmill and a hotel with the imposing name of Grand View. The small school was less impressive since it had originally been a cabin.

Snow came early, often in October, and stayed late so the little community was held in self-centered isolation. When the road was blocked after a big snowfall everything from people to bales of hay came up in the buckets on the tram line.

The miners worked long hours, seven days a week, as did their wives. All treasured the rare moments of relaxation when a missionary trudged up the trail, or a travelling theatre group performed in the bunkhouse dining room. Some of the more fortunate went to Nelson for special events, and all tried to make the Dominion Day celebrations. At Christmas the Superintendent's wife gave a big party and everyone crowded into the small schoolhouse to join the fun around a gift-laden tinselled tree.

Fredericton's life was tied to the Silver King Mine and when its veins showed signs of depletion, inhabitants prepared to leave their mountain home. The mine closed in 1902, followed by spasmodic opening. But by 1915 the Silver King was finished. Before long Fredericton had disappeared under the onslaught of heavy winter snows and lush summer vegetation.

The lonely life of pioneer miners — and often their families — is captured in the photo below of R.G. Jay at the Half-way House between Nelson and the Silver King Mine in the 1890s.

Kuskonook

Like several West Kootenay communities, Kuskonook on the east shore
of Lower Kootenay Lake flourished and died because of railway rivalry.
In 1898 the Canadian Pacific Railway was laying track westward from
Lethbridge through the Rockies in an effort to reach West Kootenay mines.
Its rival, the United States Great Northern, had organized the Bedlington
& Nelson Railway and was building from Bonners Ferry to Nelson. Late
in November, C.P.R. crews arrived at the foot of Kootenay Lake to discover
that the U.S. railway builders were already there. As a consequence, for
a few months Kuskonook was headquarters for both lines, its Wild-West
atmosphere punctuated by shooting frays, a murder and subsequent
hanging.

Young Bob Nisbet, originally from Montana, unpacked his army press
in February 1898 and set out to chronicle the stirring events of life in the
Kuskonook Searchlight. With typical frontier optimism it predicted that
Kuskonook would be Kootenay Lake's major community, eclipsing Kaslo.
Unfortunately, the prediction — and the paper — lasted only a few months.
Then Nisbet left for Kaslo to print the *Slocan Sun*.

Canadian Pacific built its wharf and transfer point at Kootenay Landing, 1 mile (1.6 km) westward, leaving Kuskonook to the Americans. At
its peak the village had 100 residents, a general store and five hotels — the
International, Klondike, Union, Butte and Kalama. When the wave of construction had passed over, Kuskonook remained the terminus for connection with the colorful Great Northern sternwheel steamers that plied the
lake. But the G.N. found that its new Bedlington & Nelson line took trade
from its Nelson & Fort Sheppard branch. In 1901 it terminated passenger
service on the new line, but it didn't really matter because Kuskonook had
burned to the ground the previous year. Population sank to ten. Some
freight activity continued but by the end of World War One that last
trackage had been torn up for scrap. In 1913 the old station house became
a store that still serves residents along the lakeshore and tourists on Highway
3A which replaced both railway and sternwheelers.

Kootenay Landing

Nearby Kootenay Landing was destined for a longer life. For three decades
it would be transfer point from rail to lake boats for passengers and freight
carried by the B.C. Southern Railway through the Crowsnest Pass to the
Kootenays. During that time sternwheel steamers and tugs plied Kootenay
Lake between the Landing and a wharf at Procter on the West Arm. As
the C.P.R. pushed its southern line westward during the summer of 1898
slips were built at Kootenay Landing to accommodate 15-car rail barges
and sternwheelers. The vessel which inaugurated the new service was the
Moyie.

She was launched at Nelson October 22, 1898, after being prefabricated
in Toronto and shipped West in some 1,000 pieces. At her launching the
Nelson Miner reported:

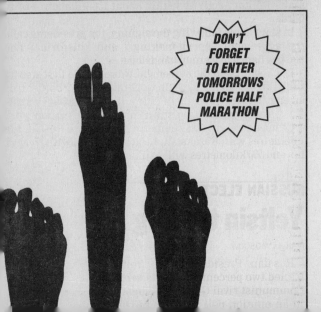

DON'T FORGET TO ENTER TOMORROWS POLICE HALF MARATHON

e a two-fold pur-
ys. The income
e local economy
ans an outlet for
cially beautiful
o give people the
st-hand the beau-
nd hopefully de-
and passion for
she says.

by spreading the
st.

y, the people and
Hertzler says. "I
uty of this coun-
n."

rried in 1960 and
1970, when they
United States to
e advantage of fi-
s. It was not until
hat the y decided
m and return to

the lodge. Mrs.
rior is rustic, but
y with a family-
offers clean com-
ated in a tropical
the lodge is the
s. Hertzler takes
pared there. Mar-

million people.

G
Foll

"Mrs. Troup broke a bottle of champagne over the bows in the most approved fashion, the ropes were cut, the newly christened *Moyie* slid rapidly and safely down the ways, and, in much less time that it takes to write it, she was slowly and gracefully on the water with her steam up and everything ready for her trial trip."

Her maiden voyage was on December 7 to Kootenay Landing, a gala

Kootenay Landing in the early 1900s. Here passengers and freight were transferred from the B.C. Southern Railway to sternwheel steamers for Kootenay Lake communities that included Nelson, below in 1897.

event to celebrate the new passenger and freight service on the B.C. Southern Railway. Aboard were newspapermen, railways officials and mayors from communities such as Rossland, Trail, Kaslo, Sandon and many others in the region. The *Moyie* was to serve three generations of Kootenay Lake residents and when her red paddlewheel turned over the final time she had plied some 2 million miles (3.2 million km) on the lake. She is today preserved at Kaslo, just the way she was when she completed her final voyage into history.

These sternwheelers played a vital role in the development of West Kootenay and for decades were the main means of transportation for residents of most communities. In a period of over 60 years, 12 of them sailed Kootenay Lake.

Sternwheelers were a uniquely North American craft, plying tens of thousands of miles of the continent's rivers and lakes. The two distinctive features were a bottom which was totally flat and a paddlewheel at the stern that required only a few inches of water. For this reason the vessels with their bluff bow could pull into a riverbank or lakeshore without requiring a wharf. The gangplank was put out and passengers and freight went ashore. The sternwheeler's ability to sail in water only knee deep is legendary, perhaps best summarized by Captain Otto Estabrooks who spent nearly 50 years sailing West Kootenay's lakes and rivers. He always assured passengers who worried about shallow water that "as long as we have a few gallons to play with we'll be fine."

The first steam vessel on the lake, however, wasn't a sternwheeler. She was the steam launch *Midge*. She arrived in 1884, brought in by promoter-developer W.A. Baillie-Grohman as part of his plan to reclaim thousands of acres of farmland at what is today Creston.

She wasn't very big, fortunately, since she was manhandled over 39 miles (63 km) of trail from Sandpoint in Idaho to Bonners Ferry, where the Kootenay River is navigable to Kootenay Lake. The task was accomplished by "a large force of Indians and some 10 or 12 white men."

The first sternwheeler to ply Kootenay Lake was the *Nelson*, launched at Nelson on June 11, 1891, by the Columbia and Kootenay Steam Navigation Company. "The boat presents a handsome appearance," noted the *Nelson Miner*, "and will take front rank among river steamers in British Columbia."

She was a "most commodious vessel . . . staunchly built, while every provision is made for the convenience of travellers. . . ." She was also colorful, with the dining and the ladies room white, boiler deck Prussian blue, and "Paris green trim on the eaves of the upper deck." Her assigned task was summarized in eight words: "Get all she could of Kootenay Lake trade."

The next vessel to appear was the *Spokane*, built by the Great Northern Railway, a U.S. line, to aid construction of its branch to Bonners Ferry. The move heralded an intense rivalry between the Great Northern and Canadian Pacific for control of West Kootenay traffic. As part of this rivalry, in 1892 a branch line was being built from Northport in Washington to Nelson. This extension was viewed with dismay by C.P.R. officials. The all-Canadian route from Vancouver to Nelson meant a trip of some 560 miles (900 km) that involved travelling by train to Revelstoke, sternwheeler down the Arrow Lakes system to Sproat's Landing, then rail again to Nelson. The trip took three days under favorable conditions, much longer at other times. The new route from Nelson to Spokane, on the other hand, was only 180 miles (290 km) with direct year-round rail access.

But competition wasn't restricted to railways. It engulfed the sternwheelers and flourished among townsite promoters. The *Nelson Miner*, for instance, carried pages of glowing advertisements praising townsites such as Lardeau, Trout Lake City, Duncan City, Argenta, Nelson, Sandon, Kaslo, Nakusp and many others.

Spurred by the development, in 1892 a third sternwheeler appeared on Kootenay Lake. She was the *City of Ainsworth*, built by the residents of Ainsworth. She was a modest vessel which didn't offer significant competition to the C.K.S.N., but a new vessel being built at Bonners Ferry was different. Her owners intended to put the C.K.S.N. "out of business."

The vessel was the *State of Idaho*, launched in April ". . . amid the booming of explosives and cheers of the populace. . . ." On May 6 she completed her maiden voyage to Kaslo, welcomed by the ". . . booming of anvils and wailing of brass bands." Unfortunately, her career was short. On November 10 she rammed a rocky shore near Ainsworth, was badly damaged and later sold to a passenger for $350.

On April 7, 1896, the C.K.S.N. launched a new sternwheeler at Nelson. She was the *Kokanee*, described as ". . . one of the most beautifully proportioned sternwheelers in the Pacific Northwest." At her launching the *Nelson Miner* reported that ". . . in all the bravery of flying colors, trim and coy, the debutante took her first plunge into the blue waters."

In November competition arrived when the *International* was launched near Kaslo. She was called a "flyer" and raced the *Kokanee* at any opportunity. She seldom won since the *Kokanee* could easily churn along at 18 miles (29 km) an hour while the *International* struggled to maintain 15 miles (24 km).

To better its competitive position, in 1896 the C.P.R. bought the pioneer C.K.S.N. It was a shrewd decision because the C.P.R. was losing out to the Great Northern. Then in 1898 the C.P.R. purchased the smelter at Trail and the Columbia and Western Railway for $800,000. It was another shrewd decision that solidified the C.P.R.'s position.

In 1897 the small sternwheeler *Marion* was shipped by rail to Kootenay Lake. Here she was put to work on the Kootenay and Arrowhead Railway being constructed at the north end of Kootenay Lake. Then in 1898 the *Moyie* was launched as part of the C.P.R.'s new passenger and freight service via the B.C. Southern Railway from Alberta.

To compete, in 1900 the G.N., through its subsidiary the Kootenay Railway and Navigation Company, launched the *Argenta* and the *Kaslo*. The latter vessel with its interior decorations of "carved mahogany and mirror plate" was designed specifically to compete with the C.P.R. This rivalry was still intense as shown by an instance in the flourishing mining community of Sandon. Both the G.N. and C.P.R. built a railway to the ore center. The G.N.'s was the Kaslo and Sandon from Kaslo on Kootenay Lake; the C.P.R.'s was the Nakusp and Slocan from Nakusp on Upper

Above: The *City of Ainsworth* at Pilot Bay. She was the only sternwheeler to founder on Kootenay Lake, drowning nine people.

The *Nasookin*, opposite, was the largest sternwheeler to ply B.C. waters. She was the pride of Nelson, always met by a crowd at the city wharf.

The *Nelson*, below left, was the first sternwheeler on Kootenay Lake. She is shown leaving Nelson in the summer of 1891.

Below: The *Kokanee* and the *Kuskanook* race down Kootenay Lake in 1908. The flat-bottomed vessels plied the lake for almost 60 years.

Arrow Lake. When the C.P.R.'s line reached Sandon and its station was completed a celebration was held. But the rival Kaslo and Sandon workmen claimed the new station was on their railway's property. During the night they tied a cable around the offending station and hooked it to a locomotive which sped off.

On Kootenay Lake, however, the Great Northern proved unable to compete and gradually lost to the C.P.R. To compound the G.N.'s problems, in 1906 the C.P.R. launched the *Kuskanook*, the largest sternwheeler yet to appear on the lake. At Nelson the mayor declared a civic holiday and a crowd of 3,500 watched the vessel slide down the ways.

She made her first trip on July 8 when she took 300 passengers on an excursion. She proved the fastest vessel yet to appear, clipping off an easy 22 miles (35 km) an hour. Her first test was July 12 when she raced the *Kaslo*. As the *Nelson Daily News* reported:

"The new C.P.R. flyer *Kuskanook* had a little race last evening with the *Kaslo* while en route to Proctor with the excursion. Nearing Busk's ranch, the *Kaslo* was sighted at a landing and she got away with a lead of about a quarter of a mile on the excursion boat. However, more coal was shovelled in and the engineer let out his engines with the result that the rival boat was quickly overhauled...."

In 1913 the C.P.R. launched an even bigger vessel. She was the nearly 2,000-ton *Nasookin*, the largest sternwheeler of some 300 that plied B.C.-Yukon waters. On April 30 she was launched at Nelson where "...gaily decorated with flags and bunting she glided gracefully and majestically into the waters of Kootenay Lake to the accompaniment of a din of whistles which drowned the cheering of the crowd...."

She was licensed to carry 550 passengers with comforts ranging from a "commodious dining room with a lofty ceiling" to promenade decks "all lighted by electricity." Of her the *Nelson Daily News* commented: "That the *Nasookin* may have a long and prosperous career should be the wish of every resident of Nelson. Her success means much to this city as well as to Kootenay and the Boundary generally. Her construction is a declaration by the Canadian Pacific Railway of faith in this country and of its intention to develop its lines through this section as a tourist and passenger route."

Unfortunately, World War One, followed by increasingly more automobiles and better roads, killed the C.P.R.'s plan to make the Kootenay-Arrow Lakes region a tourist center to rival Banff. One by one the sternwheelers were tied up and by the early 1930s only two vessels remained in service. They were the *Moyie* and the *Nasookin*, the latter purchased by the B.C. Government for use as a car ferry across Kootenay Lake. But in 1946 the *Nasookin* was replaced, leaving only the *Moyie*. She continued for just over a decade, then on April 27, 1957, made her final voyage.

By then Kootenay Landing was remembered only by old-timers. On December 31, 1930, regular passenger-freight service between Nelson and Kootenay Landing had ended when the C.P.R. extended its railway to provide a direct connection to Nelson. Today Kootenay Landing, familiar for over three decades to thousands of passengers who travelled the B.C. Southern Railway, has disappeared even from maps.

Chapter Two

LOWER COLUMBIA RIVER REGION

Fort Shepherd

Because of Kootenays' rugged topography — miles of mountains gashed by the waterways of the Columbia-Kootenay River system — the region had a comparatively small Indian population. So small, in fact, that it offered little inducement to the white fur traders to establish trading posts.

As already noted, the first was David Thompson of the North West Company. In 1807 he erected Kootenae House near the present village of Invermere in the East Kootenay and three more posts in territory which became part of the United States. It was nearly 40 years later before the Hudson's Bay Company — which had by now absorbed the North West Company — erected a post in the Kootenays, although fur brigades paddled their way up the Columbia every year on their journey of some 3,000 miles (4,800 km) to Montreal.

The post was Fort Shepherd, founded as a replacement for Fort Colville which was placed in American territory by the Oregon Treaty of 1846. The site chosen was about a mile (1.6 km) above the boundary on the west side of the Columbia River, opposite the mouth of the Pend d'Oreille. Extensive benches above the river gave flat land considered suitable for farming. Construction of the post began in the spring of 1856. By the next year two warehouses, a storehouse, officers' lodgings and quarters for the men were enclosed by a picket of tree trunks.

Known first as Fort Pend d'Oreille, the post was renamed Shepherd in 1859, presumably in honor of John Shepherd, governor of the Hudson's Bay Company from 1856 to 1858. It was never very successful. Trade flourished for a brief period in the early 1860s during the gold rush to Wild Horse Creek in the East Kootenay but shortly after the H.B.C. accepted compensation for its posts in American territory. The Fort was closed, the buildings left in the care of an Indian chief living nearby. In 1872 they burned down and Fort Shepherd passed into history.

A massive chimney was all that remained of Fort Shepherd in 1909.

Nothing has replaced it and no settlers live on the arid, chapparal-covered flat. Even today's traffic has bypassed it, following the east side of the Columbia River where a sign points to the Fort's location. At the site there is a cairn but access is by jeep road. In a way, though, the Fort hasn't totally disappeared since there is a model in Trail's Public Library.

Waneta

Gold was the catalyst which in the 1860s resulted in the first settlement of regions such as Rock Creek and East Kootenay, but not West Kootenay, although the ore of the Rossland region later yielded some $250 million worth of the yellow treasure. West Kootenay slumbered until the 1880s when roving prospectors found promising lead-silver-zinc outcroppings in the mountains bordering Kootenay Lake. The resulting boom enticed promoters and railway builders to the area. First among the latter was an American — Daniel Chase Corbin.

He had already built a railroad to the Coeur d'Alene mines in Washington, then in 1889 constructed the Spokane Falls & Northern Railway from Spokane to Marcus. Continuing northward he reached the B.C.-Washington border in 1892 and obtained a charter to construct a branch line to Nelson, a new community on Kootenay Lake. This line, incorporated as the Nelson & Fort Sheppard Railway (spelling the name Shepherd differently from that of the Hudson's Bay Company post), was built in 1893. It crossed the Pend d'Oreille River at Waneta, then followed the Beaver and Salmon River Valleys.

Bridging the Pend d'Oreille was a big job demanding the construction of a steel cantilever span 250 feet (75 m) long. The project took six months, the workmen living in a camp known as Boundary City. Honky-tonk in style with saloons, dance halls and gambling tables, it boasted 1,200 occupants at its peak. But when the bridge was finished its fate was inevitable. In midsummer 1893 construction crews began laying track northward from the border and a new community called Waneta appeared.

Waneta in its turn experienced a boom, although when missionary F.W. Laing travelled down the Arrow Lakes in 1893 conditions were rather basic. At Waneta his sleeping quarters were a roofed shack, open on three sides. His mattress was pine boards and he slept under one blanket — his own — and his overcoat. On Sunday afternoon a rancher gathered together a few people who sang hymns. In the evening a service was held in a boardinghouse.

"Tables were pushed to the rear of the room and backless benches were ranged as seats," he later wrote. "About 50 or 60 men hung around outside. The three daughters of the rancher invited them inside but it took some time before they would enter. Finally every seat was filled. The speaker stood by the stairway while a man seated on the stairs held a lamp for him. Thus was the service conducted on the frontier. The rancher is the only person in the neighborhood who professes Christianity."

When the railway was completed, Waneta didn't vanish as had Boundary City. Following railway construction came the days of the sternwheelers as they hauled supplies for smelter construction upriver at Trail Creek Landing, today's Trail. In 1896 Waneta was designated an Outport of Customs and John Nolan appointed collector. Close to the landing place was the Hotel Waneta, run by Marian Davies who was hostess to many a party given by bachelors of Trail and Waneta. Boarding the sternwheeler *Lytton* on her downriver trip, the revellers would attend a banquet and dance at Waneta, then leave on the steamer early next morning.

Optimism for the future was stimulated when placer gold along the Pend d'Oreille attracted miners. At Seven Mile the Kootenai Hydraulic Company of Rochester, New York, built a boardinghouse for the workmen and began sluicing. Unfortunately, the gold recovered did not pay the cost and Kootenai Hydraulic died.

In American territory across the valley claims were located above Cedar Creek and were acquired by International Gold & Silver Mining Company. The gold here, also, proved elusive. All that remains to recall that early boom are two 1895 gravestones among the hazelnut bushes. They lie close to the road, marking the burial place of 26-year-old Nettie Goode, wife of one of the vice-presidents, and 6-year-old D. Courtney Taylor.

As early as 1892 the first of a few settlers threaded their way through heavy forest and cleared pockets of farmland in the deep narrow valley of the Pend d'Oreille. Scattered for 15 or more miles (25 km) along the river, the families were bound together by neighborliness and religion since many belonged to the Church of Seventh Day Adventists. Their supply center was Waneta which according to a 1903 directory served about one hundred people.

The Pend d'Oreille Valley, however, was not entirely overlooked by promoters. A Spokane resident, Jack Falls, with a rosy dream of wealth, laid out a townsite at the forks of the Salmon and Pend d'Oreille Rivers. He called it Falls City. Publicity about it spread abroad and in England in 1913 Bill Guillaume left with his wife and young daughter to be postmaster in the new town. He soon discovered that Falls City existed only on paper. After spending the winter in a cabin behind the depot at Waneta, he moved to Trail where in the next 60 years he and his wife became valued and loved citizens of the Smelter City. As for Jack Falls' townsite, it never advanced beyond the promotion stage.

Another person attracted to the area was Frederick Adie. He arrived at Waneta in the early 1890s when mining prospects were bright and stayed to become its premier citizen. With a partner, Manson, he ran a general store and then took over the Fort Shepherd Hotel. For many years he was also postmaster and Justice of the Peace. As time passed and the community waned, Adie's sons moved to Trail but the Judge, as he was called, stayed until his death in 1937.

In the 1920s he sold the Fort Shepherd Hotel but it was eventually abandoned. For years it stood gaunt and paintless, its only resident John Thorell who was commonly called "Kootenay John." From some period in its career it had acquired a sign, Hotel Atoll. Beneath it someone scribbled: "No girls at all. Nothing at all."

Then in the 1950s Waneta flared into brief life. Cominco built a dam on the Pend d'Oreille River at the falls and installed a powerhouse. Construction of this $30 million project brought mammoth cranes, bulldozers and trucks swarming over the steep hillsides. Bunkhouses facing the Columbia River housed the hundreds of workmen.

Late in 1953 the 200-ft (655-m) cement and steel sluice gates were dropped and water spread up the Pend d'Oreille Valley, transforming the turbulent stream into a placid 4-mile- (6.4-km-) long lake. A highway now connected it with Trail, passing over where the old station and custom house had stood. All buildings were taken away and only a new customs house and the Boundary marker were left on the bare gravelly flat. Waneta today has a unique distinction. It is not a ghost town. It is a power plant.

Sayward

On the wide bench above Waneta the directors of the West Kootenay Land Company laid out a townsite they called Sayward. In 1901 the *Trail Creek News* stated that Sayward was desolate and only a flag station on the railroad. "There is a kind of hotel without a license run by Mr. Bauer," the paper noted, "while the only other thing of interest are hothouses owned by Mr. Fracke who has fine lettuce and radishes."

In 1906 the 1,200 acres (485 ha) at Sayward were bought by a syndicate of Rossland men. They named it Columbia Gardens and planned to turn it into a rich fruit and farming area. Water was brought by irrigation ditches from Beaver Creek and 30 farms laid out between river and railway. Settlers came from as far away as Manitoba, orchards were planted and a schoolhouse built. Unfortunately, the land proved unsuitable for fruit growing and poisonous fumes from the smelter at Trail damaged crops.

As so frequently was the case with real estate promotions, the most alluring aspect of Columbia Gardens was the name. Some mixed farming was carried on and a large dairy began operation. In the 1930s one-half of the acreage was taken over by Cominco as an airstrip for bush pilots and in the 1950s became the landing strip for the first planes flying into Trail. By then both Sayward and the West Kootenay Land Company had been long forgotten.

Erie — Craigtown — Green City

When Daniel C. Corbin built the Nelson and Fort Sheppard Railway to Kootenay Lake in 1893 he and some associates also organized the West Kootenay Land Company. Reflecting the optimism of the times they laid out townsites called Beaver (later changed to Fruitvale), Erie, Salmo and Quartz Creek, which also underwent a name change to Ymir.

There was little activity in any of them for the first four years because of the more spectacular Slocan and Rossland booms. After 1896, however, the mines above Ymir, the gold properties of Sheep Creek Valley and deposits in the mountains drained by Erie Creek captured attention and early settlements became thriving villages. Today Ymir, Salmo and Fruitvale, though small, survive because of surrounding logging and farming but Erie was not so fortunate.

It was born as a result of gold being found on the ridge between Hooch, or Whiskey, Creek and Rest Creek, and the staking of the Relief, Second Relief, Arlington and Keystone claims. Bonded to Finch and Campbell of Spokane, Washington, the Second Relief looked very promising and a small stamp mill was built. Enthusiasm ran high and on meadowland by the railway the West Kootenay Land Company laid out a townsite. Soon log cabins appeared, then two hotels and a general store built by James Hunnex who was also the druggist and postmaster. In 1899, 50 people lived in Erie and slowly increased until 1903 when there were 200. But there was also competition.

Seven miles (11 km) up the creek from Erie several claims were located at Craig's Camp, or Craigtown. Here in 1897, George McGauley opened a general store and John Bringold built a hotel. There development ended.

But such was the faith in the potential of the region that yet another community appeared. In 1899 George Green of Rossland bought the Jupiter, Ingersoll and Last Chance claims and organized the Green City Development Company. A new community planned as part of the development was called, naturally enough, Green City. Despite its grandiose name, Green City never became a rival to any place. In 1920 it had two stores and a hotel, its residential population listed as three farmers. In the late 1920s Cominco examined the property but undertook no development. Green City was abandoned, the three farmers presumably leaving. It was soon forgotten by everyone except adventurous berry pickers or autumn hunters.

The town of Erie lasted much longer, kept in existence because the Arlington and Relief claims were worked intermittently over an extended period of time. The mines were owned by various people from 1900 to World War One after which they remained idle until 1927. Two years later they were amalgamated as Relief-Arlington Mines Ltd. and in 1934 came under control of Premier Gold Mining Company. During this active period there were about 200 people in the area, most of the miners accommodated at the mine. Although fire destroyed living quarters in 1947, work continued. Small tonnages were shipped to the Trail smelter until the 1950s, but by then the community of Erie had waned. A major link to the past was severed in 1935 when storekeeper-druggist-postmaster James Hunnex retired after serving the community for over 35 years. The Mersey Hotel operated until the 1940s, although by then only 35 people lived in Erie. Today it is a suburb of nearby Salmo.

Disappearing with it were various railway sidings which handled ore from individual mines. Ten miles (16 km) out of Nelson, for instance, was Hall Siding, shipping point for mines at the headwaters of Hall Creek, with two hostelries run by Bill Doyle and John McIntyre. In the 1903 directory it is credited with 100 residents. Three miles (4.8 km) further was Porto Rico at the mouth of Barrett Creek where Louis Noel ran a store and a boarding house, surrounded by a scattering of small homes. As time passed these places also vanished, remembered only by the descendants of those pioneer miners who grubbed out an uncertain living.

Jersey City

Most ghost towns die a gradual death as their buildings are moved, collapse under the winter snow or burn down. But Jersey City's fate was unique. It died beneath the auctioneer's hammer.

Lying on a shallow bench below the skyline of Iron Mountain, the town looked down from a height of 4,000 ft. (1,220 m) to the valleys of Lost Creek and the Salmon River. Although Jersey was born in 1947, its heritage dated back to 1896 when rusty outcrops on Iron Mountain attracted prospectors, among them John Waldbeser. He staked the Emerald claim, rawhiding lead ore down the mountainside to the Sheep Creek Road and on to Salmo. Three years later he located the Jersey lead-zinc deposit and formed the Iron Mountain Company to develop the properties. Lead concentrate was shipped to the Trail smelter until 1926 when low metal prices forced closure. On the outbreak of World War Two when the mine was re-opened it was discovered that tungsten was a component of the ore. Because this metal was essential to the war effort, the Federal Government bought the Emerald and built camp buildings, a concentrator, a tramway and a new road up the steep hillside. After six weeks of operation the demand for tungsten lessened and the mill closed.

It lay idle until 1947 when Canadian Exploration Ltd., or Canex, acquired the Emerald and Jersey claims. Interest in tungsten was revived by the 1950-53 Korean War so a new mill was built and long-term contracts negotiated with the United States Government. Canex engineers examined the lead-zinc showings and drilling on the Jersey claims disclosed some 60,000 tons of good grade ore concentrated in what is called a "glory hole block." This ore was mined by open pit, giving Canex the distinction of producing two different types of ore from mines within a few hundred feet of each other by two different mining methods. Production continued until 1970 when the lead-zinc ore was exhausted, but the tungsten mill kept going until 1973.

By now Jersey City consisted of 60 company houses, a two-room school, recreation hall, mine offices and plant buildings. When Canex closed the mine the whole property was bought by Ritchie Brothers, a firm of B.C. auctioneers. They catalogued thousands of items and advertised that on September 29-30, 1973, all would be sold. In those two days 2,000 bidders from as far away as Quebec, the Yukon and California purchased practically everything in the townsite. Dump trucks, rock crushers, office furniture, mine rescue equipment, telephone switchboards, irrigation systems, truck scales, fire hydrants, a concentrator, research lab, machine shop, recreation center, 18 houses and dozens of other buildings were among items that passed under the hammer. Noted one newspaper: "The auctioneers sold everything that was on ground level or could be dragged from the 42 underground shafts."

The new owners began loading or dismantling their purchases and Jersey City quickly disappeared down the road. "The land is to be returned to its natural state after the auction," stated Canex. It was a speedy and surgical method of disposing of a community after its life had ended.

Sproat's Landing

Today Castlegar is a busy crossroads. Its airport handles jets on scheduled service while highways and railroad connect it with the Slocan and Kootenay Country to the east, the Okanagan to the west, and the American border only 40 miles (64 km) to the south. But in the pioneer era it was the Columbia River that widened to form the Arrow Lakes which brought the pioneer settlers. The first came by bateau and rowboat. Then sternwheel steamers appeared and for many years the colorful flat-bottomed vessels churned the waters some 128 miles (206 km) northward to Arrowhead on Upper Arrow Lake where connection was made with the main line of the Canadian Pacific Railway. Their landing place on Lower Arrow Lake was opposite Castlegar, close to the mouth of the Kootenay River just above a farm owned by the first settler, Thomas Sproat.

In the late 1880s several businessmen appeared at the landing place which soon became known as Sproat's Landing. R.E. Lemon, rafting a load of goods from Revelstoke, opened a store, while Bob and Sam Green who had sold supplies along the Canadian Pacific Railway during the early 1880s construction era, carried on business in a tent. There was a drug store and a stopping place, as well as stables operated by the Wilson brothers who were prominent early residents.

The original Sproat's Landing didn't live long. When the Columbia and Kootenay Railway was built by the C.P.R. in 1890-91 to provide a link between Kootenay and Arrow Lakes, a new site was chosen on higher ground. Businessmen moved away from the Landing to be absorbed into a settlement called Robson where a hotel and general stores were built near the turntable. At first a ferry transported passengers and goods across the Columbia to connect with the Columbia & Western Railway, but in 1902 a bridge was completed to provide direct access to Castlegar. Today even the site of Sproat's Landing is unknown.

The sternwheelers which called first at Sproat's Landing then at Robson have also disappeared, although for almost a century they served residents of the Arrow-Kootenay Lakes. For years virtually every community was dependent on them and generation after generation grew up, their lives governed by the schedule of the flat-bottomed vessels.

The first on the Arrow Lakes was the *Forty-Nine*, launched at Fort Colville on the Columbia River on November 18, 1865, by the "light of some candles, and fitful glimpses of the polar star." A gold rush was the stimulus — a gold rush to the "Big Bend" where the Columbia River loops around the Selkirk Mountains on its 1,100-mile (1,770 km) journey to the Pacific. With the vessel, Captain L. White intended to supply the thousands of miners who had rushed into the inaccessible area and were desperately short of food.

But Lower Arrow Lake was frozen and he had to return. In April 1866 he cast off again, this time fighting upstream 260 miles (420 km). But the Big Bend creeks quickly became known as the "Big Bilk" and the rush abruptly ended. On her third trip the *Forty-Nine* carried only three passengers.

It was 20 years before another sternwheeler churned the mountain-ringed Arrow Lakes. She was the *Kootenai* which appeared in 1885. Launched at Little Dalles, Washington, she hauled supplies northward to what is today Revelstoke to help in construction of the Canadian Pacific Railway. She operated all summer but when the railway was completed her service ended.

The next vessel to appear was in July 1888. She was the *Despatch*, but instead of having the traditional flat bottom she was a catamaran — the only twin-hulled sternwheeler ever to ply B.C. waters. Her owners quickly learned that they had no worries about a competitor copying the design.

"She was a very cranky boat," recalled John F. Hume, son of one of the owners. "The effect was like having two canoes lashed together. Another problem was that she didn't have enough room for both wood and cargo. To make time she had to have lots of wood and little cargo. If the freight load was heavy she had to stop frequently to wood up."

Despite her deficiencies, she left Revelstoke on August 8 for Sproat's Landing and successfully completed a round trip in four days. But it was obvious to her owners that she was unsatisfactory. They expanded their firm to include three prominent men — Captain J. Irving from the Lower Fraser River, businessman J.A. Mara of Kamloops and F.S. Barnard. They formed a $100,000 company called the Columbia and Kootenay Steam Navigation Company and laid the keel for a $38,000 sternwheeler at Revelstoke. She was the *Lytton*, "...built of the best material by the most experienced ship carpenters from Victoria."

She left Revelstoke on July 2, 1890, for Sproat's Landing. By now rich ore discoveries had been made in the West Kootenay and an influx of people resulted. That year Rossland and Trail were born, first of a series of communities that would include Kaslo, Sandon, Slocan, Nelson, New Denver, Trout Lake City and many others. Business was so good that the C.K.S.N. bought the *Kootenai* for $10,000 in promissary notes. She paid for herself in four trips.

Three sternwheelers which served the Arrow Lakes were the *Bonnington*, opposite page; the *Rossland*, below, whose engines could drive her as fast as an ocean liner; and the *Minto*, above. She served for almost 50 years and sailed some 2.5 million miles.

To keep pace with the rapid expansion, the C.K.S.N. ordered a new sternwheeler. She was the *Columbia* which cost an astronomical $75,000. Built at Northport, Washington, she left for Revelstoke on August 22, 1891, "...a fine looking river vessel with first class accommodation for about 40 passengers ... comfortably furnished and equipped with machinery that will send her upstream a-flying."

By now there was intense railway rivalry between the Canadian Pacific and the U.S. owned Great Northern. The G.N. wanted the ever-increasing mineral wealth of the West Kootenay to head south; the C.P.R. wanted it diverted northward to its line. To improve service in 1893 the C.P.R. started building a 27-mile (43-km) spur from Revelstoke to Arrowhead on Upper Arrow Lake to bypass a rapid-strewn section of the Columbia River.

Meanwhile, mining activity continued to flourish, as did the sternwheelers. On October 7, 1893, the *Kootenay Star* reported that on "Sunday there were no fewer than six steamers and three large scows lying at Revelstoke Wharf to load cargoes and passengers next day. These were the *Columbia, Lytton, Illecillewaet, Kootenai, Marion* and *Arrow....* Surely the trade of our port is looking up."

In December the C.K.S.N. lost the *Kootenai* when she struck a rock, but on May 9, 1896, launched the *Trail* to replace her. When she arrived on her maiden voyage the *Trail Creek News* noted:

"All the whistles in Trail made themselves heard when the ... *City of Trail* came into town.... Everyman in town who could get away from his place of business was at the landing to meet the namesake of our embryo city, and the boat received an ovation."

In 1896 the C.P.R., determined to thwart its G.N. rival, launched at Nakusp another new vessel, the *Rossland*. She was designed to make the 256-mile (412-km) return trip from Arrowhead to Robson in a day, a "real flyer" whose engines drove her faster than most ocean liners. Then in 1898 the C.P.R. added the *Minto* to its Arrow Lakes fleet. Prefabricated in Ontario and shipped West in some 1,000 pieces, she had a composite wood and steel hull which proved excellent in conditions ranging from shallow water to ice.

In 1902 some Revelstoke businessmen launched a sternwheeler to ply the dangerous waters of the Columbia River upstream to Death Rapids. She was the *Revelstoke*, a powerful vessel specifically designed for white water. Unloaded, she could sail in water less than knee deep. She successfully plied the treacherous river for 13 seasons before being destroyed in the fire which wiped out the community of Comaplix.

The next vessel to join the C.P.R.'s Arrow Lake fleet was the largest sternwheeler north of San Francisco. She was the magnificient *Bonnington* which cost an unheard of $160,000. When she was launched on April 24, 1911, Nakusp's mayor declared a half-day holiday. With "...myriad streamers fluttering and her enamel white sides gay with bunting" she slid down the greased ways and "gracefully kissed the waters of Arrow Lake." The four-deck vessel was part of a C.P.R. plan to develop the West Kootenay into a major tourist region.

World War One, however, disrupted plans. Then in 1915 the C.P.R. completed a railway via the Okanagan to provide a direct link to Vancouver.

The sternwheelers now entered their twilight years. Service on Arrow Lakes was reduced to three times a week and gradually the vessels disappeared, the majestic *Bonnington* retired in 1930. Finally only the *Minto* was left, plying the Arrowhead-Robson route on a twice weekly basis.

In the early 1950s author R.L. Neuberger wrote of her in *The Saturday Evening Post*:

"Life on Arrow Lakes is practically geared to the schedule of the vessel. Ministers time their visits to isolated parishioners to coincide with the arrival of the *Minto* at Arrowhead. Logging camps empty oil drums and larders between her voyages. Christmas packages are weighed and stamped in the tiny post office on the *Minto's* automobile deck. Prospectors keep a C.P.R. timetable in a hip pocket so they will know when the vessel will whistle off the entrance to Octopus Creek. And if a marooned ranch or bunkhouse runs out of molasses, lamp wicks or dry cells for the radio set, the supply is restored 'when the *Minto* shows up.' "

But time finally caught the *Minto*. On April 24, 1954, after nearly 60 years and some 2.5 million miles (4 million km) of service, she backed from the wharf at West Robson for the last time. With Captain R.S. Manning, who had joined her in 1911, at the wheel and flags and bunting flying, she headed north on her last trip.

At such familiar ports-of-call as Syringa Creek, Deer Park, Renata, Broadwater, Edgewood, Fauquier, Needles, Burton, Carroll's Landing, Graham's Landing, Arrow Park and others, residents waited to pay respects to their faithful friend.

At Edgewood a tearful crowd sang *Auld Lang Syne* while on the beach Jock Ford piped a lament. At Burton, citizens placed a large wreath on her weather-worn bow and at Arrowhead farmer John Nelson greeted her with an enormous sign: "Let us honor the brave pioneers of navigation on the scenic Arrow Lakes by making it possible to continue the very efficient services of the S.S. *Minto*."

At first it appeared that she would be preserved as a museum. The C.P.R. sold her to Nakusp for $1 but residents quickly lost interest. In April 1956 she was sold to a Nelson junk firm for $750. Soon they had stripped furnishings, boilers, engines, paddlewheel — everything but the hull.

On his farm up the lake at Galena Bay, John Nelson heard the news and decided that if townspeople in Nakusp wouldn't save her he would. With $800 of his slim life savings he bought the remnants of the vessel, had her towed across the lake and beached on his farm. Unfortunately, the reprieve was temporary. Because of his age and limited resources, John Nelson could do little to restore the vessel, a project estimated to cost $100,000. Then on November 26, 1967, the 88-year-old pioneer died. On August 1, 1968, so did the remains of the *Minto*.

Because of the dam on Lower Arrow Lake as part of the Columbia River project, her last resting place would soon be under water 40 feet (64 m) deep. The hulk was therefore towed onto the lake where Walter Nelson struck a match to provide a Viking's funeral for his father's dream. Grey smoke and red heat towered into the blue sky, within minutes reducing to charred remnants a famous landmark. Most of the communities she served shared a similar fate.

Waterloo

The settlement at Waterloo on the Columbia River owes its birth to perhaps the most famous of all Kootenay mining camps, Rossland. Encircled by mountains honeycombed with veins of gold and copper, Rossland poured out in such abundance that a smelter was built by F.A. Heinze, a capitalist from Butte, Montana. Organizing the British Columbia Smelting & Refining Company, he erected a smelter at Trail Creek Landing on the Columbia River some 5 miles (8 km) from Rossland, blowing in its first copper-gold furnace on February 6, 1896. Timber for fuel and smelter construction was obtained on the east side of the Columbia River about 20 miles (32 km) upstream where a landing was given the name Waterloo.

One of those supplying logs was Hiram Landis who came from the United States in August 1895. While cutting trees, Landis accidentally found iron capping in the nearby hills which persuaded him to stake mineral claims. By the following spring prospectors were striking ore on Ironclad Mountain and the north fork of Champion Creek. An English syndicate, Lillooet, Fraser & Company, took bonds on the properties and erected several buildings and a mill site. Other rich prospects were uncovered and soon the inevitable townsite appeared. It was laid out by A.E. Percival, F.W. Cowan and W. Settle who called their offspring Monte Carlo. Several restaurants served meals in tents and the log cabin Waterloo Hotel was built, while James Hunnex ran a general store. Squatters staked lots along the waterfront, and a second townsite, Montgomery, was surveyed one-half mile (.8 km) upriver from Monte Carlo.

At Monte Carlo, land clearing, street grading and building construction rapidly changed the land. Then the community's name also changed, Monte Carlo becoming Waterloo. An appropriate gathering was held at the home of Hunnex. Music was provided by the Waterloo (formerly Monte Carlo) String Band and dancing went on until daylight with a pause for a midnight champagne supper. The future seemed bright.

Two years later the brightness dimmed. The claims so hopefully bonded by the English syndicate proved disappointing and none became mines. In the spring of 1898 the company gave up its bond and by the end of the year the post office closed. Waterloo and Montgomery were deserted. Hiram Landis never lost hope and with a couple of friends kept working his prospects near Waterloo. Then he purchased 800 acres (324 ha) of land from the C.P.R., later increasing the size to 1,400 acres (561 ha) where he ranched. Presiding over all the deserted dwellings and buildings in Waterloo and Montgomery, Landis was best known as the Mayor of Montgomery.

Then in 1908 new life burst with the arrival of Doukhobors to the West Kootenay and their establishing villages on a flat they called Ooteshenie. Originally a pacifist religious sect of Russia, the Doukhobors had been living in Saskatchewan but now decided to look for Utopia in British Columbia.

In 1908 their leader, Peter Lordly Veregin, bought for the Christian

Community of Universal Brotherhood 2,700 acres (1,092 ha) of land at Waterloo and 3,000 acres (1,214 ha) up Pass Creek Valley, including Hiram Landis' Ranch. A communal organization, the Doukhobors sent a group of 80 men to prepare the place. Taking up residence in the vacant buildings at Waterloo, they began clearing the land, planting fruit trees and laying an elaborate irrigation system of wood-stave pipe. They also installed a drift-ferry across the Columbia River to a place first called West Waterloo, then Kinnaird and today South Castlegar. As a farming and settlement venture the effort was successful. By 1912, 6,000 Doukhobors had established communal villages throughout the surrounding area. Today most of these communities survive, sharing the Ooteshenie Flat with the Airport Terminal and Selkirk College. The old gold towns of Waterloo, Montgomery and Waterloo Landing, however, have vanished.

Brooklyn — Paulson — Gladstone

In the spring of 1898, the C.P.R. decided to build an extension of the Columbia & Western Railway from Robson at the foot of Lower Arrow Lake to Midway, some 100 miles (161 km) to the west in the mineral rich Boundary Country. Contract for construction was let to the firm of Mann, Larsen and Foley who picked a site on Lower Arrow Lake, 30 miles (48 km) from Robson, as headquarters, calling it Brooklyn. Equipment and supplies were brought by sternwheeler and barge while camps were established along the lakeshore so that work could proceed in both directions. A suitable pass through the nearby 8,000-ft. (2,450-m) Rossland Mountains which separate the Columbia Valley from Christina Lake had been found up Brooklyn Creek to the watershed of Dog and McCrae Creeks and down the latter to Christina Lake where Cascade City was born. Halfway between Brooklyn and Cascade the settlements of Gladstone, Paulson and Coryell briefly flashed into life then vanished into darkness when the flurry of construction had passed.

Brooklyn was situated on a point of land on claims belonging to William Parker. He had grown poor working his mining claims, but now that contractors chose his land as headquarters he had struck paydirt of a different nature. Where there had been nothing but forest his lots sold for up to $50 — an unbelievable price. Then to Parker's astonishment, they soon rose to $200 as speculators, businessmen, workmen and others flooded in from all over the Northwest. At first they had to sleep in tents or rolled up in blankets beneath the trees but shrewd businessmen from Trail quickly provided accommodation. In a month's time, J.S. Petersen had built the two-storey Crown Point Hotel. Here, according to the *Brooklyn News* which appeared five days after the town was born, customers stood in line "...as thick as editors in Paradise."

On the waterfront a wharf and warehouse were built as well as bunkhouses for the workmen, while in a stand of trees above the creek appeared a hospital containing a doctor's office, a working room and a sickroom. There was even a jail with room for a court and two small cells

Brooklyn in 1898, its main street not yet cleared of stumps.

in charge of Constable Allan Forrester. Since any trouble in the camp involved mostly liquor and fighting, the policeman's job was to handle drunks and to protect them from being "rolled and robbed." For variety, however, Forrester once had to disarm a crazed crewman on the sternwheeler *Rossland* who was threatening crew and passengers with a razor and a revolver.

Life in Brooklyn was hectic. Pounding and sawing started early in the morning, then in the evening was replaced by a different sound. Games of blackjack and poker were in session every night and bars were always crowded. For those desiring a more peaceful life, on Sundays the steam launch *Oriole* ran excursions up the lake while Presbyterian missionary John Munroe held a service in what the newspaper called the "Brooklyn Tabernacle." On weekdays, it had the less majestic title of "Reading Room" but grandly soared to the heights of "Opera House" when it housed a cyclorama of the Spanish-American War. Unfortunately, the title it assumed when the Washington Marine Band of the Salvation Army held a week-long series of meetings and concerts has been lost to history.

All through the long hot summer while forest fires filled the valley with smoke, railway construction forged ahead. The line curved along the sheer cliffs around the lakeshore, resulting in six tunnels through the rocks, five of them drilled by hand. From Robson it climbed steadily and when it reached Brooklyn was 1,000 ft. (304 m) above the town. Here it left Lower Arrow Lake to enter Dog Creek watershed and follow down McRae Creek Valley to Christina Lake. As the work progressed stopping places appeared along the route. These were shelters hastily thrown together to provide a bar where patrons could drink and roll up in a blanket on the floor — or on a bunk if extremely fortunate. In a few places, however, were establishments that were a little less basic. About halfway between Arrow and Christina Lakes, the Paulson brothers operated a hotel and stables which later became a flag station on the railway. It later acquired the name Bonanza Siding when ores from the Inland Empire and Bonanza Mines were shipped.

Four miles (6.5 km) beyond Paulson another community called Gladstone appeared when Stout & McPherson set up a portable sawmill to cut timber for tunnels, bridges and ties. It also became a center for freighting facilities and a shipping point for mining properties in Burnt Basin. Pat Burns, bringing beef to feed construction crews, built a slaughterhouse, while the Grant brothers and H.D. Hanks ran general stores beside Jim Dorsey's Gladstone Hotel, Tom Flynn's Hotel and Sam Ormond's Restaurant. Paulson and Gladstone were situated at either end of a narrow cut through the mountains which is spanned today by the Paulson Bridge on Highway #3. Nothing remains of either place, although Paulson's name is commemorated by the bridge that soars some 250 ft (83 m) over McCrae Creek.

Surviving Paulson and Gladstone for many years was Coryell, the only railway siding in that area. In 1903 it was an outlet for small ore shipments from Burnt Basin Mines. A directory listed the Grant brothers running a hotel; James McMunn, another hotel proprietor; and Wm. O'Donnell, blacksmith. In 1920 only railway section men lived at Coryell, and they disappeared when the line closed.

As for Brooklyn, its life had ended even before the railway was completed. When the construction crews moved westward they were followed by the saloon keepers and shop owners who stripped the buildings of doors and windows. In September 1899 the remains of Brooklyn burned to ashes. Only two months later a visitor "went to the spot where the town had been and then almost wondered if he had dreamed of there having been such a place."

Billy Parker's claim again became a lonely clearing in the forest, with Parker reported to be as poor as he had been before the coming of the railway. In 1910 a development company planted fruit trees on the clearing but the project failed. Twelve years later the point was bought by W. Schneider who farmed until his death in 1958. Today the farm and the site of old Brooklyn lie beneath the Arrow Lake Reservoir.

Cascade

As the railway approached Christina Lake it curved along the bluffs and gradually angled to lake level where it crossed the Kettle River on a bridge 1,000 ft. (304 m) long. Construction headquarters for Christina Lake was established at the boom town of Cascade City. Ten years previously this land had been bought by Aaron Chandler, an American from North Dakota. Organizing the Cascade Development Company, he arrived with

Cascade in the late 1890s with freight teams passing through Customs.

his agent, George Stocker, and began selling lots to enterprising businessmen who foresaw the coming of the railroad. Cascade sprang into existence with a dozen frame hotels, stores and livery stables huddled together along a wide street. A sawmill appeared, as did a local paper, church, school and hospital, with electricity coming from a power plant installed on the Kettle River. Both community and optimism flourished, the local editor predicting that "in two years Cascade City would be second to none in the entire district."

Construction of the Robson-Midway Branch of the railway began in June 1898, and in August 1899 the first locomotive chugged over the Kettle River Bridge into Cascade City. By November the line reached Greenwood and early in December an excursion party of 150 officials travelled over the scenic route. They were feted at the new communities of Grand Forks and Greenwood, with much praise accorded the C.P.R. for its great achievement in opening up the rich mining country. Everyone saw an optimistic future now that the mines of Deadwood Camp, Phoenix, Rossland and smelters at Greenwood, Grand Forks and Trail would have a Canadian outlet to the markets of the world.

Fate, however, was not kind to the towns which blossomed during the construction heyday. Shortly after trains began regular service in September 1899, Cascade City was devastated by fire. The whole center block of the main street was wiped out. Many people left and a second fire in 1901 reduced the business section to one hotel and one store. Cascade survived as a hamlet and a customs port. In 1920 it had 150 residents and a general store, but as the years passed the few buildings were torn down and it became only a port of entry on the International Boundary Line. Now only the graveyard remains — and it is hard to find.

Chapter Three

THE ARROW LAKES

Deer Park

The Columbia River Treaty which resulted in the damming of Lower Arrow Lake drowned many settlements. When the gates of the Hugh Keenleyside Dam at Castlegar were lowered in midsummer 1969, the rising waters spread over the hamlets of Deer Park, Renata, Fauquier, Needles, Edgewood and Burton, as well as hundreds of summer homes and favorite fishing holes. Buildings had been removed or burned before the reservoir was filled, while residents either had moved away or were establishing themselves in new communities above the flood waters.

Deer Park, originally an Indian camping ground, was born in the spring of 1896 when E.S. Topping and the three Petersen brothers of Trail, lured by the discovery of mineral deposits the previous fall, purchased 1,800 acres (728 ha). In 1898 when construction started on the Columbia and Western Railway across the lake at Brooklyn a boom started. The Bates brothers built the Grand View Hotel and other businesses appeared, including a bakery by Mrs. Luxton who turned out 1,000 loaves a day for the people of Brooklyn. In 1898 the original developers sold the townsite to C.H. Macintosh but it had already reached maximum development. Although railway construction was over, sporadic mining continued for a while. Farming and cutting cordwood for the Arrow Lakes sternwheel steamers provided some work and in 1907 a school was opened with 10 pupils. It was enlarged in 1912 by a group of Mennonites who also built a church. But there was little other activity, and for over half a century it was accessible only by water. Finally a road was built in 1954 but by then the community had only a few years to live before being flooded.

Renata

Although most communities in the West Kootenay were born because of mineral discoveries, Renata was surprisingly different. Renata lay on the fertile delta of Dog Creek, protected from cold winds by gently rounded mountains and watered by two creeks. It was an ideal location for fruit growing. In 1887 three French-Canadian prospectors were the first settlers and built a log hotel on the point. Afterwards nothing much changed for 20 years. Then the land was acquired by the Western Land Company of Winnipeg and subdivided for orchards. Under the management of Frank F. Siemens, its name was changed from an unofficial Dog Creek to Renata and soon the neat homesteads of 20 families dotted the flat. The first settlers were mostly of German origin — Mennonites from Saskatchewan and

Manitoba — but later people of other nationalities bought land in the area.

Individualists all and rebels in spirit, they nevertheless banded together to form a co-operative for packing, selling and shipping fruit. They also built an irrigation system, laboriously making pipes by boring holes through logs, and a sawmill to make fruit boxes. During peak years thousands of pounds of cherries, peaches, pears and apples were shipped — all by water because there was no road. After the *Minto* docked for the last time in 1954, a three-car cable ferry connected with the narrow Robson-Deer Park road.

Among the 150 or so residents were half a dozen different religious denominations, each preserving its own customs. No formal church was built but Mennonite leader, Catholic priest, Salvation Army captain, Presbyterian missionary and Lutheran minister held services in the schoolhouse. Finally, after some 50 years, the Pentecostal Assembly in 1954 remodelled a house into the Living Waters Chapel.

When the houses and buildings at Renata were burned prior to flooding, there was sorrow and regret at leaving the familiar surroundings. As they abandoned the village for new homes, citizens placed a plaque in the Robson Cemetery in memory of pioneer residents. The inscription states:

"This plaque commemorates the community of Renata and its 58 former residents who now lie beneath the water of the Arrow Reservoir."

Burton City — Mineral City — Cariboo City

For the 20 miles (32 km) between Upper and Lower Arrow Lakes where the Columbia River narrowed were several landing places — Grahams, Makinsons and Carrolls — named after settlers who shipped farm produce on sternwheelers. Here, also, were East and West Arrow Park. Connected by a ferry, they shared a school, store, public hall and St. John's Anglican Church.

The largest community, however, was Burton, born with a flourish as Burton City. It was at the lower end of the narrows, laid out about 1896 by the three Burton brothers after placer gold was found in creeks flowing down from the eastern ridge. A small rush began, the usual optimism prevailing.

As a consequence, not one but two rival communities appeared. One was Cariboo City; the other, Mineral City in the hills 7 miles (11 km) away. Here Ben Rodd built a hotel, as did Hugh and Bob Madden. Even a newspaper was planned, edited by Alfred W. Dyer. Called the *Mineral City News*, it admitted that Burton City would be the outlet for the area but claimed that "Mineral City was an ideal site, lying in a lovely valley."

But a lovely valley wasn't enough to support a town. Despite the impressive name, Mineral City was quickly abandoned. For several years Madden's hotel with its 10 bedrooms, kitchen and dining room was the family home for a miner who worked at the Chieftain Mine. In the *Nelson Daily News*, December 23, 1965, one of the children who spent two years in the hotel recalled that the "running water" was carried in buckets, mice had

Early Arrow Lake and other West Kootenay settlers frequently were victimized by promoters. For instance, the above rocky hill behind the Cotswald Ranch was sold as 40 acres of farmland.

overrun the deserted building, and the children's mother kept a light burning all night to discourage wolves.

The other community, Cariboo City, fared little better. On a flat close to Burton City, it was laid out by Sam Walker and his sister. They built the Cariboo Hotel but after a conflict with Burton City over boundary lines Cariboo City faded from the record.

Burton City alone remained, although barely. In 1923 West Kootenay author-historian David Scott spent the summer there as a youth and later wrote:

"Burton City was a street of empty and dilapidated buildings — a combined general store and post office, a community hall, a school and two churches remained in use. But we soon learned that the spirit of the metropolis was far from dead. It amused us to hear people up the creek talking about 'Going to the City,' meaning a trip to the general store. There was no access except by the steamer which called three times a week, but isolation was seldom mentioned.

"One mine on the mountain behind Burton still operated. In the tradition of the boom days the miners came to town on Saturday nights, but now all Burton City could offer for recreation was the dance in the community hall and 'bee wine'.

"This bee wine was a craze which swept the country in the 1920s. The 'bees' were the dried flowers of one of the orchis plants — fluffy white on the outside and dark yellow or brown at the core, far too much like real bees for my taste. The bees were put in glass crocks filled with water and allowed to ferment, and it was disturbing to watch through the glass and see the bees moving up and down as if they were alive. Eventually the bees sank to the bottom and the amber liquid of a very suggestive color was drained off. Bee wine was the elixir of life, and it was claimed that it could cure anything from arthritis to tuberculosis. A popular topic of conversation at tea parties was where to buy the best bees: Was it T. Eaton's, Simpsons or David Spencer Ltd.? The truth is, I think, that all of rural Canada far from liquor stores went on a mild binge with bee wine, but the fad only lasted a couple of years, then the innocuous stuff was forgotten.

"My Burton City summer has never been forgotten, not so much for the bee wine but because we had to set a splendid example since father was a Minister of the Presbyterian Church. It was the mosquitoes which remain most memorable. The community was built on low ground which jutted into the lake, flooded in the spring and slowly drained during the summer. There was a creek running through the town. This also rose in the spring and left stagnant pools when it receded. These natural breeding grounds produced the menacing mosquito population.

"We boys slept in a tent, and the ominous note in this Burton City summer was instantly apparent. Coarse green mosquito netting (69¢ a yard at Eaton's — more at the local store) was stretched over every door, window and all the beds. Mosquitoes were not just a casual nuisance in Burton City, they were a menace and a way of life. Outdoors nearly everyone wore veils of that uncomfortable netting over the face and tucked in securely at the collar. Women also wore brown paper wound around their legs inside their stockings which caused a strange rustling sound.

"Smudges were used everywhere — these were simply pails of glowing embers with grass or leaves thrown over them. At church services the congregations' praises rose heavenward through columns of smoke, but it is doubtful if it occurred to anyone that the effect was pagan. All public gatherings were held in the same atmosphere and all homes were smudged before bedtime. I was amazed to see the cloud of mosquitoes hanging just above the manse and the tent when they were smudged, and I wondered if we could survive if all the insects descended on us at once. This never happened, but getting to bed was always hazardous. In the smoky tent we blew out the coal-oil lamp, undressed quickly, lifted the mosquito netting, dived into bed and tucked the netting under the mattress again."

Despite the mosquitoes and the isolation which was common to many Arrow Lakes communities, Burton served the area for over 60 years. Then its community hall, store, school, two churches and baseball field vanished when Lower Arrow Lake was dammed. But the name survives. A quarter mile from the flooded community a new Burton arose. Its church, hall, ball park, school, stores and homes picturesquely located among the trees, it is one of the few Arrow Lakes communities to survive.

Fauquier — Needles — Edgewood

First settlers on Lower Arrow Lake either travelled by boat or followed a packtrail to Nakusp. But when a road replaced the trail in 1913, a ferry crossing over the Columbia was established between Fauquier and Needles, the latter providing access to the community of Edgewood and the populous Inonoaklin Valley with its mixed farming, dairying, pure-bred stock and poultry raising.

All three settlements disappeared in the flooding, but Fauquier and Edgewood were replaced by new towns, the residents largely the people who had previously lived in them. New Fauquier was built on a moderate slope with a magnificient northwest view. With its paved streets, community hall, boulevards, a variety of business places, school, beach, campgrounds and a golf course, it is a modern, pleasant community.

Edgewood, too, in its new setting among the trees is a pleasant community, still serving the Inonoaklin Valley and the Monashee Country, now linked to the Okanagan by paved Highway 6.

By contrast, about all that remains of Needles is a description in the book, *People in the Way*, by J.W. Wilson. According to a former schoolboy, it was a "place of criss-crossing roads, old houses, a wooden store high off the ground, a post-office the size of a bathroom, an abandoned church next to a community hall ready to fall any time, a garage, one old hotel and a school, grades 1-6." Needles lies now beneath the lake.

Also beneath the water is what once was one of B.C.'s largest hydro stations. In 1948 B.C. Hydro began constructing a generating plant 2 miles (3.2 km) north of Needles on the shore of Lower Arrow Lake, using water from Whatshan Lakes in the hills above via a tunnel over 2 miles (3.2 km) long. A mammoth project that cost $5 million, it was opened with great fanfare on June 2, 1951, and began transmitting electricity to the North Okanagan and Kamloops. But its fate was no better than a homesteader's humble log shack. It was stripped of anything movable, the remnants then gradually covered by the rising waters.

Edgewood was among communities which disappeared when Lower Arrow Lake was dammed as part of the Columbia River project.

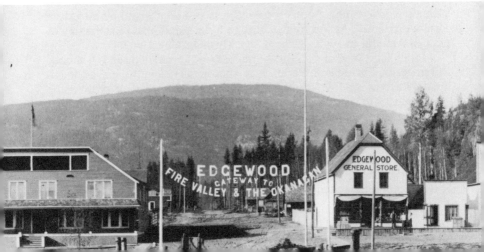

Halcyon Hot Springs

Above the narrows lay Upper Arrow Lake, 43 miles (60 km) long and up to 3 miles (4.8 km) wide. Bordered by forested mountains rising almost sheer from the water, it offered the occasional sandy beach at the mouth of a creek where woodsmen cut fuel for passing sternwheelers or lumber companies established sawmills. Nakusp, its chief town, survived the flooding but lumber camps like West Demars and East Demars, Pingston Creek and Fosthall disappeared beneath the waters, as did Arrowhead and Beaton. But two famous resorts, Halcyon Hot Springs and the Gates of St. Leon, forestalled this fate. They were destroyed by fire.

Halcyon was developed by Captain George Sanderson who in the early 1880s freighted up the lakes during construction of the C.P.R. He erected a small building around a plunge to which wooden pipe brought hot water down the hillside. Adding a stove and a well-stocked bar, he gave the place the name "Halcyon," signifying health and happiness. In 1898 the Halcyon Hot Springs Hotel was purchased by the British American Corporation when that syndicate operated several Rossland mines. Managing director was the Honorable C.H. Mackintosh who built a large addition to the original building, erected cottages for family accommodation and set up a bottling works.

Halcyon declined in popularity during World War One and prohibition days, but in the mid-1920s it revived. It was acquired by the White Cross and placed under the management of a distinguished doctor, Brigadier-General F.W.E. Burnham. Born in Ontario, General Burnham served in World War One as chief surgeon at a British hospital in Montenegro where he was responsible for organizing the White Cross of Canada which furnished medical supplies to the Balkan countries. He and his wife were highly honored by Albanian, Italian and Montenegrin Governments for their work and generosity.

Early in the spring of 1924 the General with his wife and two sisters-in-law began renovating the four-storey building at Halcyon. All mattresses were burned, old carpets taken up, new beds installed, woodwork painted and lounge and drawing room filled with treasures collected by the Burnhams on world travels. Japanese watercolors and etchings, French furniture, Viennese vases, Chinese porcelains and screen, and a grand piano gave a cosmopolitan air. At the foot of the staircase stood bronze statuettes of the General and his wife, gifts of the Albanian Government.

He built cottages and a series of hot baths where arthritic and rheumatic sufferers could be treated. For 35 years thousands visited the spa, although the only access was by water, mainly by the sternwheeler *Minto*. As the vessel pulled into the dock she was greeted by the General, two black spaniels at his heels. In the busy early years a mule called "Old Mule Jack" hauled luggage up from the wharf in a small cart. As trade dwindled the six-foot General himself hiked up the steep trail to the hotel, carrying suitcases or pulling them in a handcart.

In later years when Mrs. Burnham died he erected a shrine above her grave. It stood in a clump of silver birch trees beside a creek, 10 minutes'

Halcyon Hot Springs in the early 1900s.

walk from the hotel. Inside the gabled chapel was a Persian carpet, Buhl cabinets inlaid with tortoise shell and brass, French chairs and a needlework cabinet supposedly made for Napoleon.

Then on a winter's morning in 1955 General Burnham died in a funeral pyre that consumed the hotel and all its treasures. The 83-year-old doctor, while lighting the kitchen stove, had spilled oil and the place burst into flames. A waitress and a Japanese cook were unable to get through the blaze to the General who had collapsed on the floor. His ashes were interred in the little chapel beside his wife. Although Halcyon is gone, the hot springs remain, far enough above the lake to escape immersion.

St. Leon

Down the lake a few miles from Halcyon, a luxury resort hotel called The Gates of St. Leon met a somewhat similar fate. It was built in 1902 by Mike Grady, an Irish prospector whose claims had resulted in the rich Standard Mine above Silverton. Three-storeys high, with pillared entrance and arched balcony, it was made of cedar that weathered to a reddish brown and featured a sweeping staircase, lofty dining room and generously proportioned bar.

Sternwheelers paused at St. Leon so that passengers could refresh themselves until the captain's whistle called all aboard again. The hotel was also a popular rendezvous for loggers in the sawmills at Pingston or Arrowhead. Unfortunately, prohibition in 1917 decreased the hotel's appeal.

47

At the same time boat traffic lessened when the Kettle Valley Railway was completed. Gradually, St. Leon was deserted by the holidaying public but Mike Grady stayed. A visitor in 1921 found him living alone in the big rambling hotel which was almost bare of furniture. An old man with shaggy white hair, he remained a recluse until old age forced him to the Kamloops home for the aged. He died in 1944.

In 1945 St. Leon was purchased by Edwin B. Gates, an American chemical engineer who had acted as consultant at Cominco's heavy water plant in Trail during World War Two. Impressed by the beauty of the West Kootenay he restored the old hotel, rechristening it The Gates of St. Leon. He operated it as a resort until it was expropriated as part of the Columbia River project. Standing empty on the lakeshore, it was fated for inundation by the rising waters but in November 1968 mysteriously caught fire. Heart-broken, and suffering from arthritis, Ed Gates moved to Nakusp where he died in 1973 at 67.

Arrowhead

Arrowhead was strategically located 27 miles (43 km) south of Revelstoke where the Columbia River flows into Upper Arrow Lake. In 1893 the C.P.R. started work on a spur line to connect it to Revelstoke and when it was completed the new community became the distribution point for the entire Arrow Lakes system 128 miles (206 km) southward to Robson. It was also the supply point for the Lardeau region at the head of the lake's Northeast Arm.

By 1911 it had a permanent population of some 200 with another 300 in the surrounding area where three sawmills operated. Among buildings were a large public hall, two hotels, two churches and a City Hall.

As in most pioneer communities, a constant threat was fire. In February 1904 a blaze broke out about midnight in the boarding house of the Arrowhead Lumber Company. Evidently two dogs, pets of Company president W.R. Beatty, had upset a coal-oil lamp and the building was soon ashes. Beatty attempted to save the dogs but delayed too long and was injured by flying debris. He was taken by special train to Revelstoke where he died. A second casualty was mill manager Bill Taggart.

Just over two years later another fire swept through an entire city block. Starting in a store, the flames burned City Hall, a cigar store, the Union Hotel, the Newman Block and three houses. Ironically, a waterworks system had just been installed but wasn't quite ready.

Fire, though, wasn't the only hazard to residents. At 2 a.m. on a March morning in 1903 a 2,000-ft.- (609-m-) high slab of rock plummeted into the Northeast Arm some 2 miles (3.2 km) from Arrowhead. With a crunching roar it broke through the ice and a 6-ft. (1.8-m) tidal wave swept shoreward. It lifted the sternwheeler *Revelstoke* from its berth at the Arrowhead dock and deposited it onto the beach. Then a second wave washed her back into place.

But there were many pleasant events. On Christmas, New Year's and

A C.P.R. train and Arrowhead's main street in the 1906 era. For over 50 years the community was the distribution point for the Arrow Lakes.

other holidays sternwheelers brought isolated settlers from around Upper Arrow Lake to Arrowhead to break their loneliness and isolation. At times there was an added attraction. Once a late November snow storm caught the *Lardeau* as she pulled out for home from the Lakeview Hotel. She struck a sandbar, the *Trout Lake News* reporting that she "...danced around all night and morning found her prodding at a mudbank like a sandpiper!"

As well as fun and camaraderie, there was the frontier spirit of co-operation. One occasion was when Alex Cummins, stricken by typhoid in spring, needed medical help. Since the ice was unsafe for a team, or even a single horse, 24 volunteers roped themselves together and pulled him on a sleigh to Arrowhead.

Flooding of the Arrow Lakes inundated Arrowhead, although by then it had lost its importance since sternwheelers had ceased plying the lake in 1954, followed by closing of the Arrowhead-Revelstoke spur railway. Today access is by road along the eastern side of Upper Arrow Lake to Galena Bay, then ferry to Shelter Bay and highway to Revelstoke.

Beaton

Like a finger thrust into the rugged land of mountains, the Northeast Arm of Upper Arrow Lake provided access to the mining area drained by a river called Incomappleux by the Indians, but Fish by the miners. In the late 1880s the first prospectors to the Upper Lardeau came down the rapid-strewn Columbia River from Farwell (today's Revelstoke) to the Northeast Arm, beached their boats in protected places and cut trails through the bush. Sternwheelers later used the same landings, several ranchers took up land and a few settlements appeared.

One was halfway along the Northeast Arm. Here in the late 1890s J.W. Thompson and Malcolm Beaton took up land that became known as Thompson's Landing but in 1901 was changed to Beaton. Discovery of many mines in the hills resulted in a 16-mile (26-km) wagon track through the forested wilderness to Trout Lake City and Ferguson.

To serve the communities, Craig and Hamilton started the Pioneer Livery and Dray Stage. Although a newspaper credits the stage with holding six passengers inside, old-timer Fred Lade, who as a youth drove stage between the mining camps, knew otherwise. The stage was not enclosed. Behind the driver's raised seat was a long open box with four or five seats for 10 or 12 passengers. When it rained they used umbrellas or got wet. On the "road" it took six horses to pull the stage, the driver held in by a seat belt, his left foot wedged in a toe strap on the floor boards, right foot always near the brake.

As a transfer point for water-borne freight and passengers from the C.P.R. station at Arrowhead to Trout Lake and Camborne, Beaton enjoyed a boom. Houses, a hotel and stores appeared on the waterfront and a feeling of prosperity prevailed. Then came disaster.

On August 31, 1904, it was almost wiped out by fire. At 10:30 that Monday morning flames broke out in the Prospectors' Exchange Hotel and

Mattie Gunterman with her husband and son on the Dewdney Trail in 1898. They walked most of the 600 miles from Seattle to the Arrow Lakes. Mattie was an enthusiastic photographer whose record of life in pioneer communities is among the finest in Canada. A selection from 1900-05 is on the following two pages.

swept up the street. All buildings on the south side were burned except the Strutt house that was saved by blowing up the nearby assay office. Flames then crossed the street, burning the Pioneer Hotel and Bramford's Livery Stable. Only a few houses and the log community hall survived. Billy Boyd had just purchased the Prospectors' Exchange but with typical frontier confidence in the future began rebuilding at once. His new edifice, the Beaton, boasted 22 large rooms.

Founders J.W. Thompson and Malcolm Beaton bought the townsite in 1906. But when the price of ore collapsed in the early 1900s, Trout Lake City and Ferguson began to disappear and so did Beaton.

In 1967 Fred Lade returned to Beaton at 74 to spend his retirement in the area where, in his youth, he had worked in mining camps and driven stagecoach. Beaton was about to disappear since crews were working on the Columbia River project which would raise the lake level.

As the late Donovan Clemson, B.C. author-photographer who loved exploring provincial byways, wrote after a visit to Beaton:

"Fred acquired an old log house and moved it log by log to his property high above flood line. The 60-year-old cedar logs were sound and Fred built a cosy home which also served as the Beaton post office until it was discontinued several years later.

"There with his wife, his chickens, his apple trees and his memories he enjoyed the leisurely pace of ghost-town living. Curious visitors to Beaton were hospitably received at the Lade home, and Fred, a great raconteur,

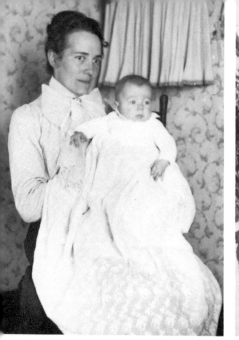

Above: Ann and Rose Williams in the kitchen at the Nettie L Mine.

Top, left to right: Mother and child in the Lardeau; hauling supplies to the Nettie L Mine; and a skating party with Mattie at left.

Opposite: The bodies of seven miners gassed at the Nettie L Mine being shipped from Beaton to their homes in Nova Scotia.

Andy Daney's freight wagon and driver "Chummy" Johnson at Halfway Creek on the narrow, winding Beaton-Ferguson road in 1902.

loved to tell of his experiences in the early days. As a youth he drove stage between the Lardeau camps and was infected with the enthusiasm and optimism of the period to the extent that he never lost his admiration for his wild country and the people who discovered and developed the mines. Fred was 10 when he came to the Lardeau and he died there early in 1976 at 83. Beaton is gone, too, covered by the flood waters when the Arrow Lakes dam was completed.''

But while Beaton is gone, it and other Lardeau communities live in a remarkable series of photos taken during the early 1900s and preserved by an incredible circumstance. The story began in 1898 when Bill Gunterman and his wife, Ida Madeline "Mattie," and their 5-year-old son arrived at Thompson's Landing. They had walked most of the way from Seattle — some 600 miles (960 km) — where doctors told Mattie that she had tuberculosis and needed a drier climate. They settled on a farm where among buildings they erected was a woodshed with an attic which served as a darkroom for Mattie who had a deep interest in photography. On the journey from Seattle she had taken many photos, her bulky camera, sheet-size plate glass negatives, tripod and camping equipment on a packhorse.

Over the years the Guntermans worked at a variety of jobs but always returned to Beaton. In the drier air Mattie's tuberculosis disappeared and she led a busy life that included cooking in mining camps. In 1927 the family

54

had the misfortune to lose their home in a fire which destroyed Mattie's cameras and photos. Then in 1936 her husband died. Mattie refused to leave Beaton and lived with her son until she died in 1945 at 73.

That would have been the last the world knew of her had not Ron D'Altroy, then curator of the Northwest History collection of photos at the Vancouver Public Library, visited the Lardeau. By chance he met Mattie's son, Henry, who told him about some glass negatives that his mother had taken over a half century before. They were stored in an old shed, Henry told D'Altroy, and had escaped the fire that burned their house. The negatives were in a room above the shed where a packrat had built a nest over them. D'Altroy was dismayed that many were stuck together by packrat urine. As carefully as if they were a bomb, he brought them to Vancouver where photographer Bill Rooseboom spent hours separating and printing them.

"The 200 or so photos are a record of pretty well every aspect of life in a mining community," D'Altroy stated. "To me they are the best collection ever to come out of a small community."

They have since been shown on TV programs, in special displays at the Vancouver Public Library and on a 15-month tour across Canada. Mattie Gunterman, a modest woman described as "a wonderful person," would have been proud that other Canadians were able to share the day-by-day life of her beloved Lardeau.

Comaplix

On Upper Arrow Lake's Northeast Arm near the mouth of the Incomappleux, or Fish, River, an attempt was made to establish a hamlet called Lardeau City. Poorly situated on swampy ground, it flooded at high water so finally gave way to Comaplix 2 miles (3.2 km) away on higher ground. Here the Kootenay Lumber Company built a sawmill which employed 40 men and put two vessels on the Arm, the *Archer* and the *Lardeau*, the latter a screw steamer with a capacity of 10 tons of freight and passengers. Soon other boats were making regular runs between Arrowhead, Beaton and Comaplix, including the *Adam Hall* for the Big Bend Lumber Company and the *George F. Piper* for the Empire Lumber Company. Comaplix became outfitting point for the Fish River district, with a general store and two hotels. In the early 1900s it was a thriving community and every year produced millions of feet of lumber.

Then in the spring of 1915 fire broke out in the lumber yard and swept over the town. It was completely destroyed, even the sternwheeler *Revelstoke* at the wharf going up in smoke. The loss included 14 million feet of lumber, stables, store, warehouse, machine shop and dry kiln, the Comaplix Hotel and 17 houses. All that remained by morning was the school, a few small houses and piles of smouldering lumber. Fortunately, no lives were lost. Afterwards the homeless residents were taken to Arrowhead, never to return.

In contrast to many communities, there was no prolonged disintegration at Comaplix. It disappeared one fiery night.

Chapter Four

THE SILVERY SLOCAN

Kaslo

Although it was the Blue Bell, the Silver King and the mines of Hot Springs Camp (Ainsworth) which lured prospectors and promoters to West Kootenay in the 1880s, it was the Slocan country between Kootenay and Slocan Lakes that made it famous. Rich outcrops lying close to the surface yielded quick returns to men handworking with pick and shovel, while the steepness of the mountains permitted access by short horizontal tunnels.

In the summer of 1891 three prospectors started the rush to what became known as the "Silvery Slocan." Shouldering their packs on the

beach where Kaslo Creek joins Kootenay Lake, they set off toward the snow-capped mountains. They were Andy Jardine from Ontario; John Allan, an American from Virginia; and Jack McDonald who had arrived via Upper Arrow Lake after wintering with a friend in the Lardeau because of deep snow. When the friend died of pneumonia, Jack preserved the body in a snowdrift until spring, then packed it into Kaslo for burial.

The three followed Kaslo Creek to its source in two small mountain lakes they christened Fish and Bear. About 13 miles (21 km) from Kootenay Lake they found a promising outcrop in a region they named the Blue Ridge because it reminded Allan of his Virginia homeland. They staked claims and registered them on July 29, 1891, first in the Slocan.

The ore samples proved very rich — so rich that by early 1892 men were pouring into the mouth of Kaslo Creek. Many braved Kootenay Lake in small rowboats but most arrived on the steamers *Galena*, *City of Ainsworth*, *State of Idaho*, *Nelson*, and *Spokane*. They pitched tents on the beach, then shouldered their packs and headed for Bear Lake Summit and the snow-capped mountains.

Kaslo about 1897 when it was the major community on Kootenay Lake. In the early 1890s it had a population of some 3,000 while Nelson had only 600.

At the time there was only one log cabin on the site, built the previous year by David Kane whose brother, George, had staked some 8,000 acres (3,237 ha) next to a timber lease owned by G.O. Buchanan. It was George Kane's land, however, not the timber lease, which proved most valuable. Once miners, promoters and others started arriving by the hundreds, Kane subdivided 160 acres (65 ha) into lots and the town of Kaslo was born. Throughout 1891 the rush continued and by 1892 Kaslo had a population of some 600 and businesses that included a newspaper, the *Kaslo-Slocan Examiner*, and was the busiest community on the lake, even if rather basic.

As the booklet *Historical Kaslo* by the Kootenay Lake Historical Society notes:

"The population was made up almost entirely of men, although a few families had arrived. There were few sidewalks and no electric lights. The streets were in complete darkness at night and people found their way about using miners' lamps or 'bugs' made from a tomato can with a small piece of candle inside and a piece of haywire for a handle. The more prosperous used coal-oil burning lanterns. There were no waterworks, so fresh water from Kaslo Creek was sold from two hogsheads on a wagon drawn by a team of horses. This was delivered daily for twenty-five cents a barrel to the downtown residents, while the unfortunate ones living out of town had to pay double that price."

By 1893 the population had jumped to 3,000, with additional thousands of transients who filled every type of accommodation. Among hotels was the Slocan. It had 70 rooms and was built by 75 carpenters in 30 days from lumber so green "the needles were still growing." To save time the foundation was nailed right to the tree stumps. One consequence of building with green lumber was that as the boards in partitions dried they shrank, and privacy in adjoining rooms grew less by the day. But this shrinkage posed no problem. Such was the demand for space that there were three customers for every bed and occupants slept in shifts.

Businesses included a bank, 14 barber shops, a variety of saloons, a second newspaper, Robert Thornton Lowery's *Kaslo Claim*, and the Comique Theatre, although a more appropriate name would have been "Red-light Theatre." The three-storey building had a saloon on each floor and a revolving stage with vaudeville entertainment. It was packed every night, not so much for the entertainment but for the 80 "dancing girls," with dancing one of their lesser qualifications.

The Comique was short lived. Respectable citizens considered it a blot on the community. At Kaslo's first City Council meeting a delegation presented a petition saying so and the establishment was soon closed.

Lowery's paper was equally short-lived. The financial center of the Slocan was Spokane, Washington, where a panic resulted in the price of silver falling and five banks failing. Money to invest in potential mines evaporated. In Kaslo the bank and other business places closed and population dropped to under 1,000. On August 25, 1893, the last edition of the *Kaslo Claim* appeared. But the irrepressible Lowery couldn't be expected to quietly "go bust." The front page was a journalistic first. On it was a drawing of a tombstone, edged in black. "Busted, by Gosh," Lowery forthrightly stated, then added: "Keep off the grass, sacred to the memory of the Kaslo Claim. Born May 12, 1893: died August 25, 1893. Aged sixteen weeks. Let her R.I.P.''

After Lowery left Kalso he moved to Nakusp and started *The Ledge*, a paper which he described as ''the leading excitement.'' In all, he founded eight newspapers during his B.C. newspaper career. Not content with the weeklies he also began a monthly periodical which he claimed ''...will be shot into the journalistic sky. The light from it can be easily seen with a dollar.'' A couple of years later he ''wrote, compiled, published and shipped a literary blend'' called *Float* which, in his words, ''tells about booze in Nelson, poker in the Silvery Slocan, gospel at Bear Lake and rain in New Denver.'' In his publications he left probably the most colorful accounts ever written about life in West Kootenay's mining communities.

Lowery was a small, bearded man who had acquired the nickname ''Colonel'' during his travels and was always given this title, although he insisted it was for ''millinery, rather than military reasons.'' He was about 5 ft. (1.5 m) tall, with spectacles and a mild manner. His outward ap-

Rawhiding ore from the Reco Mine at Sandon. In this transportation method the hides of cattle, deer or horses were filled with ore, chained together and dragged down the mountainside. At times even the horses wore snowshoes.

pearance, however, concealed an acid wit, with readers either titillated or shocked by his comments. Among those shocked were the C.P.R. which refused to allow his papers to be sold on its trains, and the clergy.

When four ministers left the church to go mining the following comment appeared in his *New Denver Ledge*:

"Four parsons have recently deserted their pulpits in Kootenay to make filthy lucre out of mining. The power of gold is indeed great when God's brokers will quit fishing for souls to bait their hooks for the stock sucker. The fact just mentioned proves how mercenary and insincere some of the western skypilots are."

In his book, *Saints and Sinners*, W.T. Moir wrote:

"I bought the whole edition (*Lowery's Claim*) and burned it in the stove. . . . He died as he lived. The strange thing about him was that he always employed printers of good character, and his old mother in the East was a Christian woman."

In addition to his talent for writing prose that could be both cutting and humorous, Lowery was an excellent poker player and a heavy drinker in an age when heavy drinking was routine. While he was the champion of the miners and others he felt had been victimized by bureaucracy or corporations, he was the despair of nurses in various hospitals where he was frequently admitted for "The same old thing."

Lowery was always ready to defend the underdog, especially miners who worked long hours in dark and dangerous mine shafts for little pay.

"The miner is the backbone of every mining camp," he once wrote. "It is upon the money that he earns that we, who live in the towns hard by, get our daily bread and other luxuries. It is for him principally that the saloons are fitted up in gorgeous style. It is for him that the storekeeper is waiting so that he may pay his bills. It is through his hard work that many men of capital are enabled to ride in carriages and dine with dukes in Europe. He gets $3.50 a day in the Slocan and for this amount he pounds a drill and lacerates rocks in the darkness of the tunnel or shaft. He occasionally is assisted up the golden stairs by a premature blast, and sometimes gets introduced to St. Peter by aid of a snowslide. Being of so much value to the community, his life should be freed from danger as much as possible. One way to do this is to have all buildings at the mines built in such a manner as to obviate the danger from slides, and render it unnecessary for men to flee for their lives, as has been done during the past week.

"Miners may be plentiful and some capitalists may think that their lives cut but a small figure, but we think different. We want every one of them to have a chance to die in bed, and we urge upon all owners the necessity of seeing that their employees are protected from the danger of slides in every way possible. Take our advice, boys, or when the slides come again some of you may have to push clouds, instead of holding the end of a drill."

After Lowery left Kaslo — and despite the gloomy outlook — late in 1893 the community was incorporated as a city, with R.F. Green its first mayor. Unfortunately, 1894 brought more disasters. On the frigid night of February 25, 1894, a fire apparently started deliberately wiped out much of Front Street with its hotels, stores and other businesses. About one-half

"Lardo" Jack McDonald and Andrew Jardine at their Beaver Camp claim in 1891. They were two of the three prospectors who started the rush to the "Silvery Slocan," in its day Canada's richest mining area.

of the community's assessed value became ashes.

With typical frontier optimism rebuilding started immediately but more problems were on the horizon. The winter had been characterized by an unusually heavy snowfall throughout the region, followed by a late spring. When the snow finally melted Kootenay Lake rose some 14 ft. (4 m) above normal high water. The region east of 3rd Street — about one-half of the area not previously destroyed by fire — was submerged in water up to 10 ft. (3 m) deep.

Then on June 3 a freak storm with hurricane-force winds struck, churning the lake into waves up to 10 ft. (3 m) high. The wharf, jail and scores more buildings were destroyed, including the Galena Trading Company's store which disappeared. The only items saved were the "barrels of liquor which were found floating in the lake." Mixed with the liquor were the remnants of houses and their contents — sofas, pianos, chairs, tables and other items.

But more was to come. The hot wind of the storm caused a heavy snow melt in the mountains and the already flooding Kaslo Creek rose higher. On the night following the storm the creek destroyed many businesses and homes, including the two-storey one of Mayor George Kane which was 90 ft. (36 m) from the creek bank. In four months some three-quarters of the city's assessed value had vanished.

Rebuilding began as soon as flood waters subsided, although many residents had to buy new lots since theirs had been washed away. Silver prices rose and the community slowly recovered. In 1895 it was given a massive boost when the Kaslo and Slocan Railway was constructed some 33 miles (53 km) to the flourishing mining center of Sandon.

In 1897 the *Year Book of British Columbia* reported that Kaslo had a "...population of 2,000 ... a splendid water supply ... and good fire protection. Kaslo is the central distributing point for the Slocan mines, seventy-five good shipping mines being tributary to it. These may be worked all the year round and at very little expense. The development work is increasing, although a mere beginning has been made. Splendidly equipped steamers run on the lake making connection with the through trains on the C.P.R., N.P.R. and Great Northern....

"Kaslo has a beautiful situation on a flat plateau on the lake front. There are numerous fine buildngs (chiefly wooden frame), churches, school house, public offices, sawmill (capacity 40,000 feet per day), planing mill, sash and door factory, ore sampling works, brewery and bottling works, two banks, electric light works, and numerous stores for miners' supplies, etc. The city is progressive, 100 buildings having been erected during the spring and summer of 1897 and municipal improvements such as sewage system, are in contemplation."

Unfortunately, the price of silver plummeted again and this time didn't recover. Kaslo began a decline, the population dropping to some 700 from its peak of 5,000. Today it is a stable community of 1,000, its economy supported by logging and the scenery and sport fishing which draws thousands of visitors a year. Its rich historical background is evident in the 65 officially designated heritage buildings, including City Hall and the Presbyterian Church, both built in 1898.

The main historical attraction is the *Moyie*, the sternwheeler which began serving Kootenay Lake residents in 1898 and continued until 1957. Although Kaslo by then had dwindled from the thriving gateway to the rich Silvery Slocan to a village of some 700, residents felt that the aging vessel should have a home in the community she had served for nearly 60 years. As noted in the book, *Paddlewheels on the Frontier — The Story of B.C.-Yukon Sternwheel Steamers:*

"The C.P.R. agreed and gave her to the village. To supervise the formidable task of upkeep and management the Kootenay Lake Historical Society was formed. Its first president was Noel Bacchus, a trapper and rancher who had forsaken a London banking career for the freedom of Kootenay Lake. His enthusiasm, supported by the Board of Trade, Service Clubs, Fire Brigade and scores of residents, resulted in $15,000 being raised to finance the first phase of the preservation project.

"Today the *Moyie* rests in a concrete berth at the end of Front Street in Kaslo. She is preserved as she was on her last trip and the policy of the Historical Society is to change nothing that will alter her appearance. Wheelhouse, galley, boilers and engines are intact and in place, even the varying tones of her whistle are preserved on a recording.

"Since Kaslo is off the main highway the *Moyie* was comparatively lonely during her first years on display. But British Columbians have a growing pride in their colorful history and she now welcomes over 10,000 people a year. In her white hull, buff funnel and red paddlewheel she is a proud symbol of an era known to fewer and fewer people."

South Fork, or Zwicky

Five miles (8 km) out of Kaslo, on a flat where the South Fork of Kaslo Creek joins the main stream, a small townsite was laid out in the autumn of 1892. According to U.S. journalist Randall H. Kemp, it was called Nashville but most miners referred to it simply as South Fork, shipping point for the Cork-Province Mine. When the C.P.R. took over the Kaslo and Slocan Railway in 1914, the settlement was renamed Zwicky after W.E. Zwicky, manager of the Cork-Province. Today, Zwicky consists of only a couple of dilapidated log cabins in a meadow above the mountain creeks.

In the new names given to the railway stops the C.P.R. honored engineers prominent in developing Kootenay mines. W.E. Zwicky, an American from Madison, Wisconsin, came to British Columbia in 1900 when he was 42. He operated the Cork-Province during World War One, and when it closed undertook to rework the old Krao at Ainsworth and the Silver Bell in McGuigan Basin. One of Kaslo's most public-spirited citizens, Zwicky served as chairman of the Victorian Hospital Board for over 20 years. In all that time he was never a patient until his last illness. Attacked by ptomaine poisoning while out in the field, he died on October 31, 1929.

Sproule's, or Blaylock

Ten miles (16 km) beyond South Fork, Jim Sproule provided shelter and food for men and horses beside a tumbling mountain stream. Known as Sproule's, it became a station on the Kaslo and Slocan Railway, but was changed to Blaylock when the C.P.R. rebuilt the line in 1914. The station commemorated Selwyn Gwillim Blaylock who in 1899 joined the Canadian Smelting Works (later changed to Cominco) as a 20-year-old graduate metallurgy student from McGill University. After his first night in Trail, however, he probably wondered how long he would survive in a Western mining community. As he later recalled:

"I had no sooner landed on the pillow when I heard a revolver shot followed by five more in quick succession. In the morning I expected to hear of murders but nobody seemed excited and I had to inquire. 'Oh, nobody was hurt. The shooter's aim was poor and a little alcoholic'."

Despite his startling introduction to the West, Blaylock remained, becoming Cominco's President then Chairman of the Board. Although the station named after him has vanished, Cominco grew into the world's largest lead-zinc smelter complex, employing over 10,000 in its various operations.

Whitewater, or Retallack

Located in 1891, the Whitewater claim was sold to J.C. Eaton for $200. Eaton sunk his pick into a vein of solid silver-lead ore which enabled him

The Kaslo and Slocan train at Whitewater Station ore platform in 1896. A few years later the community and the railway were destroyed in a forest fire.

to interest John L. Retallack, a former sergeant in the North-West Mounted Police who had become a banker-promoter. Retallack secured the capital needed to turn it into a mine, and its future was assured. In 1898 an English syndicate secured control with Retallack remaining as manager. A concentrator was built and the neighboring Whitewater Deep property was acquired by another English company.

First settlers at Whitewater were John and James Bell who started a sawmill. They also laid out a townsite and soon it included two general stores, a bakery, a laundry with bath facilities, the Whitewater and Victoria Hotels, and the Jackson House built for railway workers. Unfortunately, in the hot summer of 1910 a small blaze, which started near New Denver 13 miles (21 km) away, was fanned by high winds that carried it up Carpenter Creek Valley. Mine buildings in Rambler Basin and at McGuigan Camp went up in flames, at the Lucky Jim Mine five lives were lost and much of the Kaslo and Slocan Railway destroyed. The approaching fire was seen in Whitewater in time to enable 36 people to take refuge in the mine tunnel. They carried water and supplies and one housewife had the foresight to boil all the eggs she had. No one was hurt as the blaze roared past the tunnel portal, but concentrator, mine buildings, houses and business buildings became ashes. So hot was the inferno that rails on the Kaslo and Slocan line were twisted.

The following year Whitewater and Whitewater Deep properties amalgamated and a new concentrator, mine buildings and houses were built. In honor of the man who had been so long associated with the mine's

development, it was renamed Retallack. Over the next decade or so the property was leased intermittently but in 1943 operated again to supply demands during World War Two. But the mine closed in 1952 and Retallack was abandoned. Today, the few windowless buildings which front Highway 31A have no chance of surviving.

Bear Lake City

Cradled in a hollow at the summit of the pass, 3,503 ft. (1,068 m) above sea level, were the two tiny lakes which Andy Jardine and his companions had found full of fish and frequented by bears. They were a natural site for a pleasant stopping place and in mid-summer of 1892 a log cabin was built by F.W. Jarvis who applied for a license to sell liquor. In the clefts between the surrounding mountains the Lucky Jim and several promising claims had been staked so Gilbert Malcolm Sproat envisioned a town on the lakeshore.

Pre-empting land, he laid out the townsite of Bear Lake City and advertised lots for sale. A shanty hotel and a few other buildings appeared but Sproat's town became just one more that never materialized. The 1894 forest fire which destroyed Whitewater wiped out all buildings, and in 1897 the only evidence of a settlement was the rebuilt hotel. It was later taken over by Robert Mitchell, a Scotsman who dispensed drinks and ran a post of-

Scotty Mitchell's place at Bear Lake in 1917, the mountains still scarred from the 1910 fire which swept up the valley and wiped out many communities.

fice and store. As the mines slowed down, Scottie switched to growing potatoes and raising chickens for workmen in neighboring mines. Today, the two lakes remain. On Fish Lake is a Department of Highways Rest Area with picnic tables in a peaceful setting, little changed from that enjoyed by Andy Jardine and his companions.

Watson

On the far side of Bear Lake, rival promoters laid out the townsite of Watson. Its life was brief, although it did get mentioned in a newspaper. The reason was that in winter many of the communities were isolated for months, with life becoming bleak and monotonous. On March 25, 1893, the *Nelson Miner* noted:

"To David Bremmer and T.G. Procter belongs the credit of bringing the first boat of the season from Kaslo to Nelson. They rowed in open water, and hauled their craft over the ice. They took back 600 pounds of whiskey freight to the town of Watson."

Unfortunately, the forest fire of 1894 incinerated the few buildings and within a few years new trees and shrubs obliterated all trace of the community. When the C.P.R. re-opened the railway between Kaslo and Sandon in 1914, the station at Bear Lake Summit was called Giegerich after a prominent Slocan merchant. Today, at the summit there are no buildings, only a highway sign: ZINCTON SUMMIT 1,068 m (3,503 ft.).

Zincton

Zincton was shipping point for the Lucky Jim Mine, one of the largest producers in the Slocan. It was staked in 1892, with nine buildings, concentrator and a few cabins clustered around the railway line. The Lucky Jim was one of the longest producing mines in the region, operating until the 1950s and yielding millions of dollars. Afterwards the buildings gradually disappeared.

So peaceful is the area that beaver have returned, a nearby Stop-of-Interest sign on the highway noting:

"A BEAVER POND: Here beaver made a home for themselves and created an oasis of life for other creatures. They have dammed a stream, logged a forest, dredged canals, and built a house. Their pond, with its clear water, lush grasses, and dead trees, provides an attractive habitat for many insects, birds, and mammals. Beaver usually work and feed at dawn and dusk."

McGuigan

From Zincton, the Kaslo and Slocan Railway snaked around the sheer 1,000-ft. (304-m) face of Payne Bluffs. Before reaching the rocky ledge, the line crossed McGuigan Creek and here a siding was built to serve a large number of mines. On the steep hillside in 1892 A.S. Farwell surveyed what could well have been the province's most precarious townsite. Despite its position, a store and three hotels — McGuigan, Crossroads and Kaslo-Slocan — found perching room. Here, also, John W. Powers set up his freighting camp.

The abandoned community of Zincton, below in the 1970s, has totally disappeared.

A crew at a Slocan mine in the early 1900s. Because most mines throughout the region were high on mountainsides, often above timberline, avalanches killed many miners.

Below: The Kaslo and Slocan Railway in 1906 after an avalanche, one of the hazards which buffeted the line.

In May 1902, a snowslide swept down the basin. It swept away his stables, 16 mules and horses, wagons and provisions which Powers was readying for a summer's freighting to the mines. Fortunately, many drivers were out with their teams and only one man was killed, but wreckage was scattered along the trail. Fortunate, also, was the fact that the slide stopped short of McGuigan town.

Because of fires in summer, heavy snowfall in winter and avalanches in spring, the K & S was difficult to maintain. After the disastrous fire in 1910 that wiped out Whitewater and twisted its rails, the line's owner, the Great Northern, ceased train service. When the C.P.R. acquired the railway in 1914 they built a 6-mile (9.6-km) extension from Zincton to Parapet and abandoned the spur around Payne Bluffs. McGuigan Siding's life cycle was completed. Now only hikers, prospectors or other outdoor people visit the long-dead site of the former busy shipping center that numbered three hotels among its business places.

Three Forks

The second largest of the communities between Kaslo and New Denver was Three Forks. Situated at the junction of Carpenter, Seaton and Kane Creeks, it was a natural crossroad for both miner and railway builder. In 1892, Eli

The first house in Three Forks in 1892.

The once vibrant "Hurrah town" of Three Forks abandoned
in the 1930s and, below, vanished in the 1960s.

70

Carpenter, who had missed becoming wealthy in the staking of the Noble Five, laid out a townsite and built a stopping place on the narrow flat sandwiched between the three turbulent streams. Here, miners stockpiled ore rawhided down the mountains and it was chosen as headquarters by the Nakusp-Sandon Railway for its branch up Carpenter Creek to Sandon and Cody. Horses and gangs of workmen made it a booming place. Along with them came saloons, gambling joints and eating places. In the slang of the day, "Three Forks was a hurrah town, the place one went for a good time." It seemed that Carpenter, unlucky in staking rich mineral claims, would become wealthy as a townsite developer.

Unfortunately, the fire of 1894 destroyed the community, including the hotels — Carpenter's Three Forks, the Wellington, Pacific and Miners' Exchange. Residents took to tents and, within a month, Sam Lovatt had a sawmill in operation. Soon four new hotels appeared, as did six stores and a jail, comfortably fitted with five cells, a kitchen and a Constable's room. Bill Pratt freighted his printing press from New Denver and began publishing *The Prospector* in which he chronicled life and events in the "Pronged City" as he called it. Christmas that year of 1894 was one of great festivity. During the holiday there were three balls, in addition to a Christmas tree celebration, a wrestling match and the first wedding in Three Forks when Mrs. Dryden, who was in charge of rooms at the Pacific Hotel, married proprietor Terrill.

But after the railway was completed and construction gangs left, business slackened. Three Forks became just a divisional point. Gradually, Kaslo, New Denver and Sandon supplied the area and Three Forks' hotels and stores closed. In 1918 when George Murhart shut the doors of his hotel and store, newspaperman Lowery remarked that the famous old camp looked like a ghost city, with but a handful of old trail-blazers left. Then even they were gone. Today, there is no sign of turntables or switchbacks, no rubble from hotels or ore bins, no indication of any habitation. All that remains are the rushing waters of Carpenter, Seaton and Kane Creeks and a covered sign erected by the Valhalla Wilderness Society with the following information:

"K & S RAILWAY HISTORICAL TRAIL: You are standing in the old townsite of Three Forks near the large white false-fronted building, visible in the lower middle of the overall view of Three Forks.

"Three Forks began as a stop-over for ore-haulers on their way to New Denver. In 1894, it became the end of the line for a new C.P.R. railway from Nakusp and soon had 15 businesses, 6 hotels, and a population of 2,000....

"For a short time wagons brought rich silver-lead ore to load onto C.P.R. ore cars. However, the Kaslo & Slocan Railway was completed in Nov. 1895 to service Sandon and carry ore out to Kaslo instead. The K & S consisted of 51 km (30 miles) of narrow-gauge track coming up the valley from Kaslo and edging along Payne Mountain....

"Not to be left behind the C.P.R. finished pushing through their line to Sandon a few weeks later. No longer needed, Three Forks declined, until by 1904 only two hotels and one store remained, and the population was below 100."

Sandon

On the western fringe of what was once Three Forks a gravel road leaves paved Highway 31A and heads up Carpenter Creek to the rubble of Sandon, once a pulsating mining community that at its peak was served by two railways and included an opera house among its attributes. But, being a balanced mining community, it also had a flourishing red light district. The remains of several mines of the scores it served still scar the mountainside above Carpenter Creek, several evident during the 3-mile (5-km) drive into the ghost town.

At the highway junction an historical sign provides a sketch of what was once the second largest community in West Kootenay:

"SANDON: Today Sandon is a ghost town but there was a time when its streets echoed to the sound of footsteps and it boasted a population of 5,000.

"In the 1890s, when silver was king, 24 hotels, 23 saloons, general stores, mining brokers' offices, newspapers, a bank and diverse business establishments could be seen on its main street.

"Incorporated as a city in 1898, it remained the soul of the 'Silvery Slocan' for over half a century.

"Finally, in 1955, it was decimated by a flood which undermined the main street and left the town as it now stands."

The father of Sandon was John Morgan Harris, at the time a young man of 28. Leaving his native Virginia to seek wealth in Idaho's mining camps, he heard in 1892 of the marvellous discoveries being made in the Slocan Country of British Columbia. In the spring he set off for Nelson, choosing the approach by way of Slocan River and Lake. Prospecting brought little luck, but Harris formed a partnership with Fred T. Kelly and S.M. Wharton to purchase from a man named Ruecau claims he had stak-

Opposite page: Sandon in the 1890s when it was one of West Kootenay's largest communities with businesses that included two newspapers, five men's clothing stores and seventeen hotels. One year its team won a provincial hockey championship.

Below: In May 1900 a massive fire destroyed Sandon.

Opposite: J.M. "Johnny" Harris founded the community and lived there for nearly 60 years.

ed above the Payne Mine. The new owners registered the property as the Reco and it brought them riches.

In the autumn of 1895 Harris staked the Loudon claim at the junction of Sandon and Carpenter Creeks. But instead of mining, he formed a partnership with Gilbert M. Sproat to lay out the townsite of Sandon. Stumps were cleared, streets graded and rents collected from those camping on the creek bank. Harris laid pipe for waterworks and built a power plant on Carpenter Creek. The community quickly became the commercial center of the Silvery Slocan. City Hall, opera house, Miners' Union Building, the greatest collection of hotels in any West Kootenay community, and other buildings lined the main street with its board sidewalk over roaring Carpenter Creek. Two railways, the Great Northern and Canadian Pacific, served the community and as newspaperman Randall Kemp noted in 1897:

"Sandon is unique, with its winding narrow crooked streets and sidewalks at different elevations. It breathes life and prosperity. There is nothing lacking and everything can be had to suit any purse. People from all over the mining world jostle each other on the street or meet in the lobbies of the different hotels. An old-timer will meet friends from any camp he has been in, so need never be lonesome."

Among inhabitants was the inimitable Robert Thornton Lowery who started *The Paystreak*. His paper would, he wrote, report "mining notes taken from the hills of the greatest white metal camp on earth." In his colorful prose he also commented on a variety of other topics, noting that "Wagons laden with goods constantly arriving and pack trains departing for the hills make Sandon's main street look as animated as fair day in Ireland." When the Great Northern and Canadian Pacific tracks arrived he observed that "With two railways in Sandon the whistling of locomotives will never cease in the sunless city." (The "sunless city" description originated because the community was in a narrow valley whose surrounding mountains blocked much of the sunlight.)

Sandon's life, like its location, was checkered by sunshine and shadow, with tragedy ever present. A former resident, George Stewart, after a visit to the community wrote in *Pioneer Days in British Columbia, Volume One*:

"In the old cemetery about a mile below Sandon I recalled some of these tragedies. The cemetery itself has almost vanished, no one would find it unless he knew where it was. Trees and brush grow in profusion. There are no stone markers and the wooden ones have fallen from decay, but after cleaning away the debris I discovered the printing on some was still legible. One of the first I found was for the grave of George Chapman. A bird was painted in black on the top of it.

"An elderly man, George had a couple of rooms over a furniture warehouse. He made his living by cleaning and pressing miners' suits and raising canaries for sale. A fire started in his quarters one night after he had retired. When the fire was brought under control, the building was pretty well demolished. On an old-fashioned iron bed in a reclining position were the charred remains of old George.

"The next boards I uncovered were almost together. One bore the name of Sheppard; the other, McFarlane. Sheppard was 28 years old and McFarlane 30 when they both died on March 5, 1898. The two men worked as partners at the Noble 5 Mine, two miles above the town. To reach the mine they had to cross a large slide area known as the Bluebird. One day as they returned an avalanche swept over them. Volunteers came from Sandon, Cody and the surrounding mines to dig but not for several days did they find the bodies of the unfortunate pair.

"A great many miners lost their lives in the Noble 5 slide. The Noble 5 camp was built in a safe place but the men had to cross the slide to reach the tunnels. Annually it took its toll, sometimes one a year, sometimes two or more. One December a young Welshman, Tommy Thomas, and four Italians were swept to their death. They were killed on December 24. Young Thomas had planned a farewell celebration in Sandon that night before leaving on Christmas Day to go home to Wales.

"The next tragedy was personal. In the 1930s almost everyone in Sandon was on relief and had no money for such things as fuel. Everyone therefore cut his own wood. Most of the woodcutters were careful not to cut trees on the steep hills directly above the houses. This was especially true in the draws where there was grave danger of snowslides starting. But some people were thoughtless and among the trees they cut were some in a little draw directly above my father's house. This annoyed Dad because he was always worrying about the consequences if the trees were cut.

"At the time my wife, two little girls and I lived about 300 feet further up the gulch. Our eldest girl, Evelyn, had just started school and had a constant companion in my brother's Alsatian dog, Rex. He would escort her to school each day, and at noon and after school sit on the road watching the gulch. When it was time for Evelyn to come home he would hurry off without being told to meet her.

"The snowfall that depression winter was very heavy; at times the road connecting Sandon with the outside became impassable because of deep snow and slides. On the night of February 22 it began to snow heavily, with two feet of light fluffy snow falling on the hills and town. Then the weather turned mild and slides began to run.

"At noon on February 24, Rex went to meet his playmate as usual and I walked part way home with them. Evelyn always had lunch at her grandmother's but as we neared their home a snowslide thundered across the road not far above my house. Alarmed, I stopped to watch it, while Evelyn and the dog continued on. A few moments later I continued on my way. What made me look up the hillside I will never know, but there bearing down on me was a snowslide. With a terrifying roar and massive wind it swept past, enveloping me in white. Fortunately, I was on the edge and escaped uninjured. An old fellow, John McLeod, had a cabin nearby and he ran out. I told him to give me a shovel — my little girl was in the slide. I took the shovel and was running back when I heard him shout. Looking up I saw another massive slide — tons of snow, trees, and other debris rumbling down on me. Again I was forced to flee. Then all was still.

"I began to scramble over the snow and debris, then suddenly realized that my father's house was under tons of snow. Running toward the back, I saw the kitchen was still standing, though badly twisted. As I looked I saw my wife and my mother crawling over the snow near the woodshed. Dad also had survived, but Evelyn was buried under tons of snow.

Opposite page: City Hall with flood rubble in 1958 and a fire hydrant being reclaimed by the forest.

Opposite: The Last Chance Mine at Sandon with workers on the tailings dump. Some mines were so high that buildings had to be fastened to the mountainside.

Below: The rebuilt Sandon in 1918. It was destroyed a second time in 1955 when Carpenter Creek washed most of the community into Slocan Lake.

"All the townspeople were quickly at the scene and old men, young men, women and children began digging. J.M. Harris, founder of Sandon and owner of the Sandon Light and Water Company, strung wires and erected floodlights to enable work to continue during darkness. By 11 o'clock that night everyone was exhausted and all went home — not to sleep, but to rest. Lights shone from most homes all night. Early the next day volunteer crews arrived from New Denver and Silverton. There was no means of transportation since the roads were blocked, but these men had waded in snow to their knees the whole way, some of them for 13 miles. The citizens took them into their homes and fed them, then they started the gigantic task of tunneling into the 25-foot-deep slide in search of our 6-year-old daughter. I never left the scene. At 10 o'clock on Friday a workman came and said they had found her. She lay against a chair where the dining room had been. We did not find Rex until June."

In addition to avalanches, there were floods and fires, including one on a May evening in 1900 that wiped out the community. No lives were lost but in the grey light of morning, 1,000 homeless gazed at the smouldering ruins. With typical frontier optimism, rebuilding started when the ashes cooled.

Unknown to residents, however, Sandon was doomed. Ore prices fell in the early 1900s but revived during World War One. Then at war's end came another slump, followed by depleted ore bodies and the 1930s depression.

There was a reprieve during World War Two when the B.C. Government, alarmed at the presence of Japanese along the coast, moved them to the Interior. One thousand Japanese men, women and children were sent to Sandon to fill the empty houses. This influx revived the community, although only briefly. At war's end the Japanese left. Population dropped to 100. Buildings stood boarded up, only the Reco Hotel open for business. There in the large hostelry with its shiny furniture and bright flowers lived elderly Johnny Harris and Alma, his handsome energetic wife.

Now in his eighties, Harris was frail but managed to tend the power plant on Carpenter Creek which had provided light for Sandon since he installed it in 1896. Then on a December day in 1953 Johnny Harris died at 89. To many people he was synonymous with Sandon — in early years as its most prominent citizen, in later days as the courtly white-haired symbol of its colorful past.

Sandon did not long outlast its founder. On a wild night of storm in 1955 it died. Torrential rains devastated the Kootenays and already swollen Carpenter Creek burst its flume wall and poured tons of rocks and debris on the town, literally buffeting it to pieces. The main street's board sidewalk was torn out and carried away. Hotels and stores on the edge of the creek were undermined then carried downstream to a massive raft of debris which formed in Slocan Lake. When the flood subsided the boulder-strewn town was only desolation. One woman remarked: "It's good Mr. Harris isn't here to see his town go!"

Sandon never recovered. The shell of the Virginia Hotel and the City Hall, built in 1900, still stand, but little else. Sooner or later — probably sooner — they will join the hundreds of other ghosts of Sandon.

Cody

One mile up Carpenter Creek from Sandon was the settlement of Cody. Here beside the tumbling waters of Cody Creek Tom Mitchell built a mill to treat ore from the Noble Five group of mines and on a few acres of flat ground a small townsite was laid out. John M. Winter built a two-storey hotel which accommodated 50 guests, followed by a second hotel run by W.E. Terril, while A.B. Docksteader operated a general store and post office. Population reached 100 and in 1897 journalist Randall Kemp predicted a great future. "As a town," he said, "Cody will probably never have a rival."

He was right. Every spring, slides and avalanches swept down Cody Mountain, carrying men and horses to their death and demolishing mine buildings. Somehow Cody escaped destruction but many a time the road to Sandon was carried away or the train blocked by snow. Because of the constricted valley, mine workers preferred living in Sandon. By 1903 only one family, the Winters, remained.

Mrs. Winters had narrowly escaped death when the railway coach she and her child were in broke away and ran down a grade. Fortunately, both were unhurt. But in late November 1903 even the Winters joined the exodus. The Noble Five Mine was worked intermittently until the 1950s, but by then Cody had long been only a memory.

Alamo Siding

Another settlement spawned by mine and railroad was Alamo Siding. It was 4 miles (6.4 km) from New Denver at the junction of Howson and Carpenter Creeks. Built on a rocky spur above the creeks, it consisted of post office, store, manager's house, bunkhouse and concentrator for treating the ores of the Alamo and Idaho Mines which were 6,000 ft. (1,830 m) high at the headwaters of boulder-strewn Howson Creek. By 1904 population was about 200.

In 1916 Clarence Cunningham took over the Idaho-Alamo Mines and another old one called the Queen Bess. It proved as rich as a winning lottery ticket since he uncovered ore which yielded a net profit of over $1 million. He replaced the old mill at Alamo Siding with a new one costing $250,000 and acquired many old mines in the Slocan. Unfortunately, he was never able to duplicate his Queen Bess winnings.

Open-handed, free and easy, Cunningham became a well-known figure as he rode along the trails on Rex, his big chestnut horse. One day Rex accidentally broke his master's leg, crippling him for life. Then depression years brought financial reverses and the Cunningham enterprises became burdened with debt. When he died in 1938 his affairs were so complicated that it was 11 years before they were straightened out.

As time went on, Slocan ores went to Trail for concentration and the Alamo mill closed. In 1951 the railway was abandoned and Alamo Siding reclaimed by the forest.

Chapter Five

SLOCAN LAKE

New Denver

Slocan Lake is a beautiful 24-mile- (40-km-) long waterway cradled in the deep cleft between the Valhalla and the Selkirk Mountains. In the boom days of the 1890s when the Silvery Slocan was the most famous mining region in B.C., its eastern shore and surrounding mountains were the locale of a variety of settlements. Of them, only three survive — New Denver, Silverton and Slocan City.

New Denver was the first, dating to December 1890 when four pro- spectors — Long, Hunter, Evans and Henderson — arrived at the south end of Slocan Lake. From there they rowed 20 miles (32 km) to a delta on the lake's east shore. Hurriedly erecting a log cabin on the creek — later christened Carpenter — they prepared to spend the long winter in what they called Eldorado.

By April they had been joined by about 500 others. Although most headed into the 8,500-ft. (2,600-m) mountains that towered around the lake as soon as weather permitted, others remained.

They changed the name Eldorado to New Denver after a mining com- munity in Colorado and laid out a townsite. Soon business places included six hotels. The community owed much of its prosperity to the Bosun Mine, 3 miles (5 km) down the lakeshore. Here on a ranch owned by a young Englishman, Joseph C. Harris, a prospector discovered rich ore. Several months' work paid for a road, wharf, and blacksmith shop, as well as pro- viding funds for a waterworks system in New Denver and the Bosun Opera House.

New Denver became a major supply center and in 1893 even became something of a port. That summer lumber for a 60-ft. (18-m) steamer, the

William Hunter, was cut by hand on the beach and her boiler, two propellers and other ironware brought by packhorse from Nakusp. Although she was described as "hand-sawn and homemade," she received the traditional launching, her owners, the Slocan Trading and Navigation Company, liberally providing "drinks and cigars." She plied the lake on a regular basis, carrying freight and passengers to the various landings. She tended to be top heavy, a design flaw that on one occasion caused her owners some embarrassment. As she left New Denver those on board crowded to one side to wave to their friends. The weight unbalanced her and she rolled over. Fortunately, her passengers were merely dunked and not drowned.

In 1897 the *Year Book of B.C.* listed over 20 business places in New Denver, among them five hotels, two drugstores, two furniture stores, tobacco store and an undertaker., One of its citizens was the wandering newspaperman, Robert Thornton Lowery. After going broke in Kaslo he had moved to Nakusp where in 1893 he started the *Nakusp Ledge*. He remained there just over a year and in December 1894 moved to New Denver because of the "financial frost." His paper now became the *New Denver Ledge*. He promptly christened his new home "The Lucerne of America," noting that "Paradise is the only rival to the little town where the *Ledge* dreams away its life."

As had happened at Poplar and Kaslo, Lowery left behind a colorful account of life in a mining community. Little escaped him, especially if it involved the local hotels and saloons. Here is an item from an 1896 paper:

"Popcorn Jim, accompanied by a band of box-car tourists, alighted in New Denver last Saturday and immediately commenced to paint the town a crimson shade. Popcorn attempted to run the bar at the Windsor but Dad Black ran him out with a poker. He then proceeded to the Newmarket and

New Denver on Slocan Lake in the late 1890s.
The hotel near the beach is the Newmarket, above,
built in 1893. It was to serve the community
for 80 years, burning down in 1973.

had one of his pals tell Stege that he was the worst son of a female canine in the mountains. The bluff did not go with the Newmarket Landlord, and Popcorn, after insulting several people, was chased out of the hotel by a baseball club in the hands of the landlord. Stege got in a home run on Popcorn which put him out on the first base. This howling tough from Toughville next raided the Central Hotel along with his pal and ordered Dan Cronin to put up the drinks or fight. As Dan once went through a torpedo boat explosion a small event like this did not bother him. He merely reached over the bar and staked a claret location on the nose of Popcorn's pal which made that individual's face look like a summer sunset during the forest fire season. Satisfied that Dan was shift boss they wandered elsewhere. . . . ''

In 1897 there was a dramatic change in the transportation system. In February the C.P.R. bought the Columbia and Kootenay Steam Navigation Company which had pioneered sternwheel service on both Arrow and Kootenay Lakes. At the time the C.K.S.N. had a sternwheel steamer, the *Slocan*, under construction at Rosebery north of New Denver. She was launched in May 1897, a speedy vessel with excellent accommodation. That same year the C.P.R. completed an extension of its Columbia and Kootenay Railway from Robson to Slocan City at the south end of the lake. The C.P.R. also bought the *William Hunter*, intending to use the Slocan Lake route as an alternative to its Arrow Lakes system, especially during low water and in winter when ice was a problem. Slocan Lake communities now had daily service to the C.P.R.'s main line at Revelstoke via Nakusp and Arrowhead.

For the communities along Slocan Lake the future seemed assured. But falling ore prices and depletion of mines created the same "financial frost" that had caused Lowery to move his paper from Nakusp to New Denver. In 1904 he again had to pick up his type and head elsewhere, this time to Nelson.

New Denver waned until World War Two when Japanese were evacuated from the Coast and sent inland to communities that included New Denver. After the war logging increased when technology made timber at higher elevations available, and logging is still the principal contributor to the economy. Today, with a population of 750, New Denver is the largest of the Slocan Lake communities. Its past lives in the Silvery Slocan Museum in the Bank of Montreal building which dates to the original rush. Outside the building is an historical sign:

"NEW DENVER: This was the town first known as Eldorado, later came New Denver when it was forecast it would become greater than its name sake, Denver, Colorado.

"By 1893 New Denver was established as the Western gateway to the silver country. Close by, silver-lead properties like the Mountain Chief, Alpha, California, Alamo and others contributed to the general prosperity of the town. To the east, Sandon, Whitewater, Three Forks, Cody and other mining towns beckoned.

"Today the original Bank of Montreal and a dozen other buildings from the turn-of-the-century stand as mute reminders of the days when this town was considered the New Eldorado.''

Rosebery

Rosebery was a small but active transportation center on the Nakusp and Slocan Railway a few miles north of New Denver at the mouth of Wilson Creek. Connection was made here with steamboats on Slocan Lake and a concentrator built to handle ores. In 1917 the Rosebery Surprise Mining Company acquired this mill, enlarged it and treated ore from the Bosun and Surprise Mines. For some years about 100 people lived and worked in Rosebery but the concentrator proved unsatisfactory so the ores were shipped to Trail. The mill buildings, houses, hotel and station have all disappeared.

Silverton

Four miles (6.5 km) down Slocan Lake from New Denver, a camp sprang up to serve the rich mines on the southern face of Idaho Mountain. Christened Silverton in honor of the famous mining town in Colorado, lots were put on the market in the early 1890s and it soon had a population of 500. Among business places were four hotels, three general stores, druggist and a newspaper, the *Silvertonian*. Founded in 1897 by druggist R.O. Matheson and his brother, Henry, its pages preserve a rich lode of Silverton's daily life. Here are a few excerpts from 1898:

"The prospects for the permanency and solidity of Silverton as a business and mining center were never as good at any time as the present. Steady development work has been going on in the surrounding mines and the old standbys have all improved with work and depth. Several new properties have been added to our list of mines. The amount of ore that will be shipped from Silverton this winter will be a surprise to the outside mining world and Silverton will rank next after Sandon as the big camp of the Slocan. Our businessmen who have been farsighted enough to see the possibilities of this camp will soon be reaping the golden harvest that their pluck and staying qualities have made them deserving of."

"H.W. Youmans of Revelstoke was in our city on Sunday evening last, exhibiting his acetylene gas generators. The light furnished by this gas resembles very closely the light of day, making the oil lights around seem sickly and yellow in comparison. The cheapness and convenience of acetylene gas recommends it to all. We understand that Mr. Youmans has received several orders in Silverton."

"Colonel Lowery, the genius of the *Ledge*, is contemplating the publication of a monthly magazine in Rossland. The issue will be brought forth under the name of *Lowery's Golden Claim*. We hope the Colonel will strike a pay-shute on the surface and never find the bottom of it."

"Our attention has been called to the fact that of late someone has been using the lake front near the Hog Ranch as a dumping ground for garbage of all description. In addition to the tin cans, which we credited to the proprietors of the Hog Ranch, we are told that the refuse from the town is dumped there. The attention of the authorities should be called to this fact and the proper steps taken to stop it.''

"Christmas night McKinnon's hall presented a view most pleasing to the eye, and the program rendered by the little ones produced in the audience a timely spirit of 'Peace on earth and good will toward mankind.' The children furnished the program complete with the exception of the music which was furnished by Messrs. Webb, McFarlane and Horton.

"Each of the little performers were greeted with a hearty round of applause as they finished their parts, but little Harriet Daigle, George Barry, George Horton, Inez and Alice Calbick and Mary Horton are deserving of special praise for the masterly manner in which they carried out their different parts.

"Two trees had been neatly arranged, one on each side of the platform, and were well loaded down with presents of all descriptions, and at the close of the exercises Santa Claus, represented by R.O. Matheson, assisted by Ross Thorburn and Mr. Horton, began the distribution of gifts, and the room was filled with merry laughter from start to finish. After a vote of thanks was tendered the committees for the happy termination of their efforts in connection with the evening's entertainment, the floor was cleared, and a couple hours was pleasantly spent in dancing.''

The Victoria Hotel and Silverton's main street in the late 1890s.

"The ball given by the Independent Order of Forresters of Silverton in McKinnon's hall New Year's Eve was a grand success, both socially and financially. Over fifty couples attended and dancing was kept up to late in the morning. Many outside people attended. The Denver people came over in sleighs, on account of a part of machinery of the steamer *Denver* — which had been chartered for the occasion — breaking soon after it had left the dock, and could not make the run.

"The hall was tastefully decorated, and the Forresters are to be congratulated on the manner in which the ball was conducted. The music was furnished by Messrs. McFarlane, Webb and Horton.

"The supper was served at the Selkirk hotel, which had been decorated for the occasion. Over the door was the following: 'Welcome I.O.F.,' and the walls were decorated with evergreens and flowers. The supper itself was a feast for the gods, and showed that Messrs. Brandon & Barrett, the proprietors, know how to please their guests."

The *Silvertonian* survived six years. During this time Silverton was kept prosperous by mines such as the Alpha, discovered by Irish prospector Mike Grady. In 1894 he began packing ore to the Silverton wharf from the Alpha Mine and became wealthy, later investing his money in the luxury hotel at St. Leon Hot Springs. (See page 47.) The adjoining Emily Edith claim became a shipping mine in 1899 but about 1905 the vein was traced to the nearby Standard. This property proved to be the biggest producer in the Slocan, bringing great wealth to George Aylard and associates. During World War One the mine employed over 200 men, including an entire concert-touring Welsh choir who were in Silverton when their funds ran out.

In the early 1900s mining started to wane and so did Silverton, although it never joined the list of vanished communities. Today it is a pleasant lakeshore village with a population of some 250. Its links to history include a 1904 general store and Civic Park with an excellent display showing one of the *William Hunter's* propellors, mining machinery, and tools used for hand drilling in mine shafts. A text notes:

"Shortly after the turn of the century rock drilling became a premier sport in the Slocan, particularly in Sandon on Labour Day and Silverton on July first.

"In 1912 Algot Erickson and Joe Johnson of Silverton teamed up and went on to win many events, including the world championship in double drilling — 8-pound hammer."

Hand-drilling rock in a mine was brutal work, done by either one man or a two-man team. A miner who worked alone, his only light a candle, used a four-pound hammer to hit the steel rod. This work was called "single-jacking." Two men working together, one holding and turning the steel rod, one using an eight-pound hammer, was called "double-jacking." With a swing of the eight-pound hammer every second, or 3,600 swings an hour, experienced men could drill through 40 inches (1 m) or more of solid rock in 15 minutes.

An excellent description of a miner single-jacking is contained in the book, *Old Silverton*, by John Norris, published by the Silverton Historical Society:

Rock drilling contests were a feature of holiday celebrations throughout the Slocan and other regions. The opposite photo shows Algot Erickson, who won a world championship, turning the steel with A. McGillivray hammering.

Mining was brutal and dangerous work. For years the only light in the tunnels was a "bug" — or candle in a pail — carried by both horses and men.

Photos from *Old Silverton*, courtesy Silverton Historical Society.

"Walking along a tunnel in a big mine, only a small portion of the track ahead illuminated by the candlelight (the carbide lamp, although invented, had not yet taken the place of the candle in Silverton mines), one could hear the muffled tap ... tap ... tap of the hammer hitting the end of the drill-steel, as some miner in a nearby stope patiently bored into the hard rock. Since stoping was usually done upwards, he held the steel above his head and in striking it had to counteract the force of gravity. There he worked ten hours a day, seven days a week, a mole slowly burrowing along the darkness of his tunnel. After each blow of the hammer he gave the sharpened bit of his steel a slight turn; the rock fragments it chipped out fell onto his face, and the sharp dust particles it ground free drifted down into his lungs, so that one day a few decades ahead he would die an agonizing death by drowning, unable to get his breath through the liquid that filled his inflamed chest."

In cemeteries throughout the Slocan and other mining regions are the graves of scores of miners who died prematurely, the mines that hastened their deaths themselves tombstones to a bygone era. As John Norris notes in *Old Silverton*:

"The story of Old Silverton can fittingly be ended at the Great Depression, because when that catastrophe was over and prosperity returned, it returned to a different world. Halted by the collapse of money, man's aggressive and expansive spirit lay dormant for nearly a decade. Like a drugged giant, the landscape lay idle, waiting to be revived by another war. In the Slocan mining camp, a greatly diminished population lived out as best it could the hard times. Life in the towns slowed nearly to a halt; smaller communities disappeared forever. In Silverton buildings stood vacant with their doors and windows unlocked, places where children could play. In the hills, cabins were left by their owners as if for an absence of a few days — cups and plates on the table, newspaper folded on the chair, wood ashes in the cook-stove. Slowly they began their return to the earth. The narrow and untrodden trails that led to them were scattered with forest seeds.

"Now, half a century later, when those seeds have become forest trees and the snows of many winters have had their way with the cabins, sometimes an unsuspecting wanderer, finding himself looking through a crooked doorway or a shattered window frame at a furnished interior that appears to have been abandoned only yesterday, will utter exclamations of amazement echoing those of the diggers who first saw the vanished world under the ashes of Pompeii.

"In the canyon of Four-Mile Creek and elsewhere, the mills, the bunkhouses, the drys, and the cook-houses waited for the return of better times until, far-away owners having lost interest, the watchmen were discharged and these buildings too began the slow process of disintegration. The revival of the Mammoth Mine just before the Second World War, although it brought a new period of prosperity to Silverton, did not affect the older mines, which continued their decay. Today almost nothing remains of them; even the tramlines have returned to the forest, their towers and cables collapsed and buried, only vertical strips of cottonwoods and aspens among the dark firs of the hillsides still showing where they had been."

Vevey Landing

About 5 miles (8 km) above Slocan City, Twelve-Mile Creek attracted prospectors and two free enterprisers called Allen and Cory. Convincing themselves that the creek had a rich future, they laid out the townsite of Vevey Landing on the lakeshore. They built a hotel and a store and operated a ranch nearby. For a time the community flourished, with C.P.R. lake boats calling regularly. Then the mining boom faded and so did Vevey Landing. While the community has been forgotten, the name lives in Vevey Creek high in a fold on Mt. Aylwin.

Enterprise City and Aylwin City

In the summer of 1894 Bob Kirkwood and J.L. McKinnon, while hiking over the divide from Cody to Slocan Lake, found rich ore near the headwaters of Ten-Mile Creek. They staked the Slocan Queen and Enterprise claims, then brought supplies by boat down Slocan Lake and packed them 8 miles (13 km) up a rough trail. Later they bonded the claims to J.A. Finch of Spokane who cut a good trail and shipped ore to a smelter. With his nephew, George Aylard, as manager and Bob Covington as foreman he built offices at the minehead and a wharf and ore shed on the lakeshore. Two settlements appeared, Enterprise City on Slocan Lake with a store, hotel, blacksmith shop and a few other buildings, and Aylwin City, some 8 miles (13 km) away high in Enterprise Basin.

Here hotelman Charlie Aylwin built a boardinghouse for the 30 or so men who worked at the mine and named the community after himself. A general store appeared, and Billy Koch built a sawmill and stables for his horses which transported the ore. In 1899 the Finch syndicate sold the Enterprise Mine to London & British Columbia Goldfields Company for a reported $750,000. After erecting a mill and working the mine for a brief time the company leased it to Billy Koch on a royalty basis. He made ore shipments for a few years but then became involved in sawmill operations and the mine closed. Over the intervening years the Enterprise has yielded ore to several operators but Aylwin City and Enterprise City, the two communities to which it gave life, are unknown to all but a few old-timers.

Oro

High in the ridge drained by Lemon Creek, the townsite of Oro was laid out at the junction of the Second Fork (Crusader Creek) with Lemon. Falls in the river supplied power for a sawmill and also a 10-stamp mill, while two hostelries provided accommodation. A pack trail led to Slocan City and a 5-mile (8-km) wagon road in summer and a 12-mile (17-km) sleigh road in winter provided access to Nelson on Kootenay Lake. In 1900 some 50 men were mining in the vicinity but when the mines were exhausted Oro disappeared. Its cabins for many years provided shelter to hunters and fishermen hiking to mountain lakes but they were eventually flattened by winter snow.

Slocan City

Slocan City in 1897 with sacks of silver ore on the dock.

At the south end of Slocan Lake, two rival communities were born during the early 1890s. They were Brandon and Slocan City, about a mile (1.6 km) apart. For a time there was keen rivalry between them but Slocan City was the only one to survive — although barely.

The townsite was founded by Frank Fletcher of Nelson, with interest in the area so great that men stood in line waiting to buy lots. Slocan City soon developed into a typical mining community, hotels with their crowded bars the most common buildings. As Fred J. Smyth who worked there as a newspaperman in 1896 recalled in his book, *Tales of the Kootenays*:

"...it was a hummer. The hotels were jammed full and everybody seemed to have plenty to spend.

"Those who could not get beds slept in chairs and on pool tables.

New Denver's Silvery Slocan museum in the early 1900s Bank of Montreal building preserves some of the region's history.

Everyone was pepped up and overflowing with optimism. Mineral claims were being staked by the hundred on Springer and Lemon Creeks, and mining deals were made every day in the week. Many went out on snowshoes and staked ground even without bothering about finding mineral in place.

"Bonds on claims for $10,000, $20,000 and $30,000 were common, and with a down cash payment of from $1-5,000. No wonder money was plentiful. Those getting their first payments spent their money freely in most cases on the assumption that within a few months another cash payment would be made."

One of the most optimistic citizens was D.R. Young, owner of the *Slocan City News*. As Smyth recalled, Young "was long on promises, but short on cash, and at the moment was broke. So was I. Thus, on the latter point, we had much in common. But he was an affable individual, bubbling over with optimism. He had the gall of the devil, and had never heard of the term 'inferiority complex.' I rather learned to like him. His greatest dread was payday, and many a Saturday night 'the ghost' failed to walk. His daily prediction was that within two years Slocan City would have a population of 15,000, and believed it, and for a time it looked as though he might be right."

In 1897, especially, Young's optimism seemed justified. On December 6 that year the first train rolled into the community over an extension of the Columbia and Kootenay Railway from Nelson. It was part of a plan by the C.P.R. to make Slocan Lake an alternative route to Arrowhead and its trans-continental line at Revelstoke. As the southern terminus, Slocan City seemed to have a secure future. But the winds of change blew unfavorably. The ore in surrounding mines was not so rich or extensive as elsewhere in the Slocan. Then came the Klondike gold rush and falling ore prices. Slocan City began to wane and soon buildings were being torn down.

Today Slocan has a population of a few hundred with logging the mainstay of the local economy, a sawmill dominating the once lovely beach fronting the community. Residents, however, have one consolation — Slocan still lives, unlike others along the lake which disappeared long ago.

Chapter Six

GHOSTS OF THE LARDEAU

Lardo

To the northwest of Kootenay Lake is the Lardeau Country, a region characterized by mountains towering over 9,000 ft. (2,743 m) and glacial streams thundering into narrow, heavily timbered valleys. Its two main waterways are the Duncan and Lardeau Rivers which join a few miles above Kootenay Lake. After the confluence of the two mountain waterways, the Duncan flows into Kootenay Lake through a large delta, although some 25 miles (40 km) of its waters were stilled by a dam built as part of the Columbia River Treaty in the 1960s.

The southern Lardeau was accessible from Kootenay Lake, the northern part most accessible from Upper Arrow Lake. But it was so remote that not until the early 1890s did news of mineral finds draw attention to it. As a result, early in 1893 a wave of prospectors were ploughing through the deep snow which covered the region. The annual report of the Minister of Mines for 1893 noted:

"In the early spring much excitement was caused in the West Kootenay district by the report of rich strikes.... At one time it was reported that as many as 300 men were camped at one place on the Duncan River awaiting the disappearance of the snow...."

As prospectors fought their way up the valleys, then struggled up the mountains to above timberline, they found extensive veins of mineralized rock. Behind them came the townsite promoters, each visioning his fledgling community as a major metropolis. In the wilderness new names appeared — Gold Hill, Gerrard, Poplar, Trout Lake City, Circle City, Ferguson, Duncan City and Goldfields, among others. Typically, the most enduring aspect for most of them would be their name.

The first was Lardo on the west shore of Kootenay Lake about a mile from the north end. It was born because both the Canadian Pacific and the Great Northern Railways had been attracted to the Lardeau by rich strikes of gold and other ores. Both companies began to push a line up the wilderness of the Duncan and Lardeau River Valleys, the C.P.R. on the west bank of the Duncan River, the Great Northern on the east bank.

In 1893 Nelson surveyor C.W. Busk, with enthusiasm typical of the area, had laid out Lardo townsite. When construction began on the C.P.R.'s Kootenay and Arrowhead Railway, it consisted of four houses and a few tents. But construction crews brought life and four hotels quickly appeared, as did a newspaper, the *Lardo Reporter*, and a depot on the lakeshore where sternwheelers landed. Population reached 200 and the townsite promoters employed 50 men clearing lots.

But Lardo flourished only briefly. Within a year both railway companies realized that the riches of the Lardeau had been exaggerated and

The sternwheeler *Kokanee* and the Arrowhead and Kootenay train at Lardeau in the early 1900s.

stopped work. The result was summarized by the *Lardo Reporter* on July 24, 1893, when its eighth — and final — issue appeared:

"The publication of a newspaper in a town containing four houses and two tents is obviously not a remunerative one.... The publishers will henceforth be compelled to refrain from issuing a paper at Lardo and will wrestle elsewhere for a winter's grubstake."

Lardo, however, didn't totally vanish. The C.P.R. finally completed its railway, although not as originally planned. It was extended 33 miles (53 km) to the south end of Trout Lake, less than one-half the way to its original destination of Arrowhead south of Revelstoke and the main transcontinental line. Nevertheless, Lardo became the point where freight and passengers bound for the Lardeau transferred from sternwheel steamers to the train.

In October 1903 one of the passengers was newspaper editor Robert Thornton Lowery, the legendary "Colonel of the Kootenays." A staunch foe of the C.P.R., he was not impressed with services provided for passengers. He later wrote:

"Passengers getting off the boat at Lardo City frequently walk into the water, owing to the way in which they have to reach the cars from the warehouse on the wharf. The lights are so dim that a firefly would not feel ashamed of their competition, while every official is dumb and so cannot tell strangers to beware of the drink. The night we passed up the line, two passengers camped in the aqua pura. The first was a clerical looking personage with only an umbrella for baggage. He stepped into three feet of the lake, and came out with a faded curse upon his lips and two feet clinging to socks that stuck to him like a sucker to an ace in the hole. In the car on the way to Poplar, he sat in stoical misery, for he dare not take his boots off for fear of flashing the intelligence that his socks were not eligible for Noah's craft when it ran on the high seas just before the boom struck Mount Ararat. The other chap was a man of immense proportions and a gentlemanly and dignified presence. He went into the drink with such force that his dignity was thrown into convulsions. With true British spirit, he commenced to swim although only in three feet of water. A judicial gentleman came to his rescue and in a moment he was on planka firma. He was wet to the collar, and certainly got it in the neck. On the way to Poplar he removed his garments and dried out. Up to date, the C.P.R. has not arrested him for indecent exposure. Both these men were sober, and the C.P.R. should reimburse them for the shock to their nerve centres and the damage to their clothes to say nothing about the horrible torment of being joshed by every fiend in the land about walking on the water.''

Lardo remained the transfer point for over half a century. Probably the biggest change in this period was its name which became Lardeau. It remained part of the Lardeau's transportation system until 1954 when a road was completed from Kaslo to Trout Lake. The next year, after over 60 years, Kootenay Lake sternwheel service ended. So did the usefulness of Lardeau.

Duncan City, or Howser

The Canadian Pacific and Great Northern Railway lines, after following separate banks of the Duncan River, converged at the foot of Duncan Lake where the roistering camp of Duncan City appeared. Original locators of the townsite were John and William Simpson who built a hotel and a general store. Soon business places included nine hotels, a bakery, brewery, laundry, a sawmill, and even a policeman when Constable Young was moved from Lardo. The C.P.R. offered storekeeper Simpson $50,000 for the townsite, but he refused, feeling it would be worth millions. The railway firm didn't agree and by-passed the community. It was the end of Duncan City, although it lingered for decades before finally disappearing.

Like Lardo, it acquired a new name — Howser. The reason was described by Billy Clark, a pioneer resident who arrived in 1907. In the book *Where the Lardeau River Flows*, one of the B.C. Government's Sound Heritage Series, he noted:

"A land company from Winnipeg bought up fruit land around the country and was selling it at $72 an acre. They used to send advertisements over to England and they even had agents over there selling land. That's how we came to know about it. An awful lot of people came out to this country in them days, all wanting to make a fortune in fruit and they didn't.

"It was tall standing timber when we came. We had to clear the land ourselves. We all had 10 acres or 20 acres apiece on the big flat and scattered all around the lake. The name of this was Duncan City in the early days.... Our post office was Duncan Lake and all the mail used to go to Duncan on Vancouver Island so they changed it to Hauser and then all our mail went to Bowser. And we got it changed to Howser which is the name today...."

Howser continued as a tiny hamlet in a majestic mountain and lake setting and became home for a few young Englishmen like Billy Clark who planned to raise fruit and vegetables. On the far side of the lake, Tim Ainsworth and his friends mingled hunting and fishing with orchards and gardens, while farther up the lake the Matthews brothers ran a farm until tragedy befell them. A marauding bear, wounded by one of the Matthews, mauled him fatally before being killed. The other brother cut his hand while skinning the animal and died of blood poisoning.

Another ranch was established by the three Hincks brothers. Formerly military men in England, Major Tom and Captain Henry had been officers in the Imperial Army, while Commander Jack Hincks had served in the Royal Navy. They raised cattle which were transported by water down Duncan Lake and then overland to Meadows Creek Station on the C.P.R. When World War One broke out the brothers returned to Europe, leaving their property in the care of Billy Clark. After the war no Hincks returned and their elaborate gardens and buildings fell into decay and were overgrown by bush.

Meanwhile, Billy Clark had settled on a flat stretch of ground at the foot of Duncan Lake. When the trees came to fruition he and his compatriots boxed apples and rowed across the lake to sell them in Simpsons' where they were shipped to mining camps in the Lardeau. Decline of mining brought loss of markets so Clark switched to other ways of earning a living. In winter he ran a trapline and, interested in prospecting, he staked many claims. With his friend Joe Gallo he traced a vein of lead and zinc running along the eastern shore of Duncan Lake and together they located the JG claims which they sold to Cominco. These formed the nucleus for the Duncan Lake Mine which was almost ready to go into production in the mid-1960s when a dam was built on the Duncan River as part of the Columbia River project. The river became a 25-mile- (40-km-) long reservoir. One by one the old-timers moved out. Houses, cabins, barns and the general store were torn down. In 1967 the settlement of Howser vanished beneath the jade-green waters of Duncan Lake.

Billy Clark, although a mild-mannered man, became bitter when he was forced to leave. "I'm to be drowned out," he exclaimed. "Just like any gopher."

Gold Hill and Bosworth

These two rivals were near the second railway crossing of the Lardeau River. Bosworth was 4 miles (6.4 km) from Howser, while Gold Hill was 3 miles (4.8 km) farther. Neither amounted to much more than a hotel and a few other buildings.

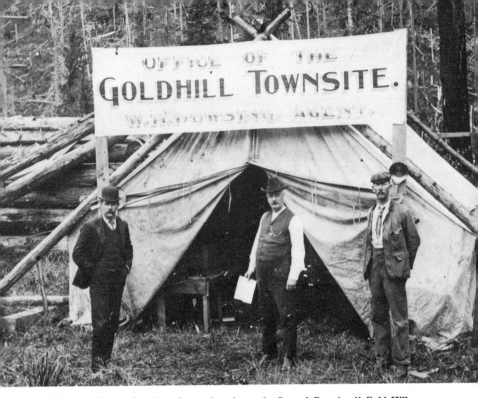

Although advertised as "...the coming city at the Second Crossing," Gold Hill never amounted to much more than the promoter's office and the Miner's Hotel, below in 1930. By the 1950s it and Gold Hill had disappeared.

Boswell's hotel opened with a flourish on New Year's Day in 1904, owners Casey and Murphy celebrating the event with a swan dinner. The Hawthorne brothers built a general store and post office. Afterwards Coloonel Lowery in his *Poplar Nugget* wrote that the community was "...beginning to put on city airs. The train stops there whether you flag it or not."

At Gold Hill, a community advertised as the "...coming city at the Second Crossing," John Ulvin built the Miner's Hotel. But that was about the end of the "coming city," even though Lowery advised readers to "Keep your optics on it." Twenty years later Gold Hill was listed in a directory as a mining and lumbering center with 15 residents, but Bosworth was mentioned as merely a flag stop with half a dozen farmers and no hotel.

In 1941 the Miner's Hotel at Gold Hill was still catering to the public with John Ulvin's daughter, Erma Rear, as proprietress. By the 1950s it, too, had succumbed, its pile of weather-worn boards Gold Hill's epitaph.

Poplar

Poplar Creek, also referred to as Poplar City, Poplar Creek Camp and plain Poplar, was located on a turbulent stream that joined the Lower Lardeau River about 15 miles (25 km) above the head of Kootenay Lake. It was born in 1903 when three prospectors, finding nuggets "large enough to hang your hat on," staked a claim they called Lucky Jack. The *Kaslo Kootenaian* newspaper noted that gold particles were "sticking out in plain sight all along the lead" and that "one can leave the cushions of the passenger coach on the A & K Railway and after a stroll of half a minute be upon the ground claimed by the locators."

The Lucky Jack lay less than 100 yards (91 m) from the Arrowhead

Newspaperman R.T. Lowery, the "Colonel of the Kootenays." The yellowing pages of his newspapers contain Canada's most witty, caustic and authentic descriptions of life in frontier mining communities.
Opposite: Poplar and the Arrowhead and Kootenay train, probably in the summer of 1903.

and Kootenay Railway (a branch of the C.P.R.) which ran from the head of Kootenay Lake to the foot of Trout Lake. Scores of other claims were quickly staked, and a store built on the creek. By September the townsite of Poplar Creek had been laid out.

Three months later the community had its own newspaper, *The Nugget*. Its purpose, stated editor-owner Robert Thornton Lowery, was to tell "the world about the glories of the new El Dorado."

In his first issue he noted: "As a rule we like to get into a camp before the pianos and canary birds, but on our arrival last week we found these things had preceded us, in addition to a large number of birds that are not canaries. The camp is a little over 100 days old and has six hotels, five of which are producing every day, four stores, a livery stable, a laundry etc., and more gold in the hills around the burg than we have ever got close to since we first planted a set of stakes in the shadow of the grand old mountains of the Great West. So, seeing that Poplar was in need of a paper to make known its wonderful resources and fight for its rights, we have hoisted our flag on the banks of Poplar Creek and printed upon it the immortal words of Macbeth. *The Nugget* is small but like the camp from which it hails it will soon grow so large that all the world can see it without straining their eyesight."

He was outraged to discover that the C.P.R. hadn't built even a shed to protect passengers and freight from the elements. As he noted:

"It is true that corporations have no soul and also true that Canada and the Canadians were created for the C.P.R. For months the world has talked about Poplar, and thousands of people have visited the camp. The town at present has five hotels and about fifteen other business houses, but the C.P.R. has not even a shed, or a telegraph instrument in the burg. Freight and baggage are dumped in the rain, while passengers use the shelter of trees for a waiting room. When the people tap the right brand of wisdom,

they will not stand for such treatment. It costs a dollar to ride 23 miles from Kootenay Lake to Poplar, and the train officials are courtesy personified, but they have no vaccine that will prevent profanity or keep sugar dry when it is set out in rain.''

The first issues carried advertisements for several hotels:

"The Poplar Hotel . . . is the oldest hotel in Poplar and adjoins the Canadian Pacific Railway depot. The wet grocery department contains pure goods, any brand of which will produce optimistic results.

"Armstrong & Almston.

"The Kaiser House . . . is convenient to the depot and has accommodation for 50 quiet guests. The nerve-bracers in the bar are free-milling and an orchestra provides music while the guests are at dinner. The landlord has studied human nature from Brazil to Alaska and knows the way to make a stranger feel at home.

"Fred Kaiser, Proprietor.

"The Royal Hotel . . . has cocktails for the nervous, beer for the delicate, whiskey for the hardy mountaineer, and cigars for those who prefer narcotic to alcoholic stimulants.

"August Buffalo, Manager.

"Hotel Inn . . . the only hotel in town that is plastered. Rates $1.50 a day and up.

"Hanson & Ostby.''

"Poplar can boast of the nicest little Swede waiter girls in the world,'' Lowery noted, in offering his personal comments on the hotel service. "There is Gussie at the Grand who smiles on all alike, whether they are 'star' or otherwise; Ole at the Inn who affects the intellectual, wears glasses and is too bashful to speak; Martie at the Dominion, a new arrival who will get the grub to the table on time even if the soup does occasionally go down the customer's back.''

In January 1904 *The Nugget* reported: "School will open in Poplar next week if the furniture arrives. J.J. Cameron is moving his school plant from Lardo here. Mr. Cameron is perhaps the only man in Canada who is owner of a complete school outfit. When school was opened in Lardo some years ago he had to put up cash for all necessary furniture. As he has never been re-imbursed for his outlay and as Lardo has about run out of population he has decided to move his school plant from Lardo to Poplar where it will run full time.

"The schoolteacher is expected on the Wednesday train. There is no necessity for young men appearing at the station in their best. She will, sooner or later, have to become accustomed to them in their digging clothes.''

On June 10, 1903, school owner J.J. Cameron and his wife became parents of the first child born in Poplar. In Lowery's words: "They are the proud possessors of the most valuable nugget yet found in the camp. It is a boy and tips the scales at ten pounds.''

Lowery also commented on the state of religion in the new town: "Rev. George Findlay of Ainsworth went up on Wednesday's train to Trout Lake where he will preach and then go to Camborne for Sunday services, returning next week. Missionaries in Kootenay have to work two shifts on weekdays and three on Sunday while the sleek, chicken-fed parson in the East has nothing to do but look wise and say 'Gee' and 'Haw'.

"The church is the only 'bust' business in Poplar. While we support seven saloons not even a parson can negotiate three squares daily. It can be said of western mining camps: 'Before the Lord erects a house of prayer, the devil builds a dozen taverns there.' "

Lowery exuded optimism about the future of the settlement. "Poplar and Paradise are similar," he commented. "Both have gold in the streets, although the latter place beats us out on angels.

Arthur G. Johnston, proprietor of the Poplar Creek General Store, the Grand Hotel and postmaster, was one of the last businessmen in Poplar. By the 1970s, below, the community had virtually disappeared.

"Prosperity is pushing Poplar pretty well past the pessimistic period. Push, pluck and perseverance are bound to win out.

"The people of Poplar can now render medical, surgical, notorial, horological assistance to everyone requiring it for we have a physician and surgeon, watch and clock manufacturer, notary public, drug store, post-office, record office, meat market, grocery and clothing stores."

Early September was brightened by an unusual celebration. "Last week there were 'doings' in this burg," Lowery wrote. "It was one of the occasions on which every prospector drops down from the hills to spend a few days. There does not appear to be any prearranged time for these gatherings. It is just a 'swarming' time. On Monday without any apparent reason for it, the Rapid Creek contingent quit work and came to town. Tuesday, Poplar Creek commenced to move, the disturbance extending as far up as the Spyglass and on Wednesday, Tenderfoot, Cascade and Meadow Creeks began to move. On Thursday the town was pretty well filled with prospectors. Before Sunday there will probably not be a single prospector in town. It is strange that men working over a district, without any prearranged plan, will quit work and gather at a common centre within a few hours of each other. This frequently occurs in a mining camp.

"An alcoholic wave hit the camp," he noted, "and many there were who fell by the wayside. There were Gaelic and French and Swede and Norwegian and Dutch and Italian and United States so badly tangled up in the atmosphere that the dogs took to cover and Charlie Hanson's bear had convulsions. Justices of the Peace took to higher levels and Chataway's mules retired to seclusion on the banks of the Tenderfoot. And yet the supply of exhilarants is more than equal to the demand."

As the year wore on, the editor's tone became less jaunty. At one time he remarked: "Although business does not appear very brisk, eight pack animals are kept busy every day taking supplies to creeks. The town seems dead but the hills are alive with men working claims."

Unfortunately for Poplar, the claims didn't result in mines and the community waned. The Colonel left in October, waving a sad farewell to the former "Paradise":

"This week *The Nugget*, editor, printer, pressman and devil, hies himself to the railroad track and takes as nearly a southern course as the transportation companies have furnished for the convenience of those who work for the public and take their pay in the next world...."

Poplar disappeared from the mining scene but continued for a number of years as a small logging center. In 1920 Charles Hanson was still running his hotel, now known as the Commercial. Helen Johnston, daughter of the storekeeper, ran the Grand Hotel and 50 people resided in the community. By 1941 the population had dwindled to 25 and by the late 1950s the forest had taken over.

After he left Poplar, the Colonel moved to Nelson, Fernie and, in 1906, to Greenwood. He published his *Ledge* in all four communities, calling it "the oldest mining camp newspaper in British Columbia." He died of dropsy in 1921 at the age of 62.

By then, many of the mining communities that he knew so well, including Poplar, had preceded him.

Gerrard

When the C.P.R. disbanded the Arrowhead and Kootenay Railway in 1928, service between Gerrard and Trout Lake City was with a Ford truck equipped with flanges. Officially known as Motor Car 600, residents soon nicknamed it the "Noble 600." It served until 1941 when the railway line became a road.

Two years after the Canadian Pacific and Great Northern abandoned their lines up the Duncan River, the C.P.R. resumed construction. But instead of terminating at Duncan Lake it was to be extended 33 miles (53 km) to the south end of Trout Lake. Here R. Green of Kaslo promptly laid out a townsite which he called Selkirk City.

When the C.P.R. moved in, however, they had plans of their own. They also surveyed a townsite but for some reason had difficulty in deciding on a name. They first chose Duchesnay, honoring one of their senior surveyors. Then it became Twin Falls. Finally they settled on Gerrard, the name of a banker in Kaslo.

In 1901 the tide of construction enveloped Gerrard as Gus Carlson, who had the contract for the work, put 500 men on the job. Slab-sided hotels were quickly thrown together. Cameron and Fulmer built Hotel Anderson; Ed Mobbs ran the Lennoxville as well as a general store; while Nils Roman, captain of the steamer *Victoria*, erected the Riverside. The original log Pioneer Hotel which had been built by Bailey and Murphy was given a second storey and a big bar of polished cedar.

In June 1902 the last spike was driven and trains began running from

Lardo to Gerrard. Here passengers and freight were transferred to the *Victoria* and *Idler* for the journey up Trout Lake to Trout Lake City. Although Lardeau now had connection with the outside world, rejoicing was brief. Heavy snows and a frozen lake forced closure of the line during winter. No great mine ever materialized in the Lardeau and production of ore was not large enough to make the railway profitable. Service was reduced to three trains weekly during the summer, none in winter. In 1917 the C.P.R. took its boats off Trout Lake and in 1928 replaced the locomotive with a truck fitted with flanges to run on rails. In 1941 even this jitney was abandoned. The rails were lifted and the right-of-way became a road.

Gerrard dwindled. In 1920 it still had a sawmill, a fish hatchery which had been established by the government, and two hotels. By 1928, population had dropped to 18, one hotel — the Gerrard — a general store, and a caretaker at the hatchery. By 1948 there were only six residents, no hotel and no hatchery. Today Gerrard has disappeared even from the B.C. Government's official road map.

Trout Lake City

Sixteen-mile-long (25-km) Trout Lake lies in a deep cleft between the glacier-topped mountains of Lardeau and Duncan Ranges some 30 miles (48 km) above the north end of Kootenay Lake. During the 1890's excitement, prospectors combing the high, scarred peaks found rich pockets of gold and silver. So extensive was the mineralization that several communities appeared, among them Trout Lake City, clustered between the tumbling glacial waters of the Upper Lardeau River and the ice-blue lake.

Spurred by the prospects of rich mines and a railway, Trout Lake grew quickly even though at first the only access was via the lake in summer and over the ice in winter. Soon the community had five hotels, a water system, a branch of the Imperial Bank of Canada, two general stores, phone system, six-bed hospital, a large Oddfellows Hall, a stage line to Beaton on Upper Arrow Lake, sidewalks, and a newspaper, the *Trout Lake Topic*. It even had a skating rink with hockey avidly played by both men and women. In fact, it and nearby Ferguson had Ladies Hockey Clubs with playoffs between various teams.

Population reached 300, with additional hundreds of miners and transients. Its future seemed assured, especially since everybody was certain that the Kootenay and Arrowhead Railway would be extended from Gerrard along Trout Lake then to Upper Arrow Lake. But in the early 1900s the price of base metals dropped and with it any hope of a railroad. Mines closed and so did Trout Lake City. One resident, however, refused to leave.

She was Alice Elizabeth Jowett, a remarkable pioneer who lived in Trout Lake for over half a century. She was born in 1853 in England, and at 25 was left a widow with four young children. She decided to try her fortune in Canada and in 1889 sailed for Vancouver. Alice Jowett established a bakery and for seven years turned out pies and cakes, bread and buns. Then, with an urge for change, she sold her store and moved to Trout Lake

The remarkable Mrs. Alice Jowett was 94 when the photo opposite was taken. The same year she experienced her first plane ride and insisted on being flown over her claims in the mountains. She had previously inspected them on horseback every year until she was past 80.

Below: Her Windsor Hotel in the early 1900s and Trout Lake City's decaying main street in 1946.

City. With only an Indian woman for help she operated a hotel in a log cabin, her excellent cooking soon resulting in a profitable business.

Across the road from her log cabin hostelry was the Windsor Hotel, a large three-storey frame building with dormer windows. Her own place quickly became too small and in the late 1890s she bought the Windsor.

Under her management the Windsor became known far beyond the Lardeau. Luxuriously furnished, its fittings included a bar and a billiard room. Its dining room gleamed with silver flatware and white tablecloths, while Alice Jowett's roast beef and Yorkshire pudding gladdened the hearts of all its guests. Those guests came from far-away places — New York, Dublin, Goteborg, Johannesburg, Coolgardie in West Australia, and all the towns in British Columbia. Some of the visitors were famous people, including W.C. Van Horne, president of the C.P.R. Many a miner holidayed at the hotel, giving as home address the mine where he worked. Consequently, the register abounded in colorful place names: Free Coinage, Bad Shot, Rawhide Trail, Circle City, Rabbit Creek, Horseshoe, Nickle Plate. On January of every year added comments were supplied by celebrating miners describing their friends: Sinner, Barber, Butcher, Hobo, Methodist, Dusty Simon, Rubber Neck, Stiff, Dead Bum, Coyote Ketcher, Hasher, Swamper, Masher.

Once established in the Lardeau, Mrs. Jowett soon caught the prospecting fever and began to hike into the hills on a search for claims. Riding horseback she explored a ridge at the headwaters of Ottawa and Eight-Mile Creeks near the summit of Silver Cup Mountain. Here she located the Foggy Day, the Arralu, the You and I, the Alpine and the Hercules, prospects which she leased for working. Mining became a passion and she attended conventions in Nelson and Spokane, while visiting engineers and geologists were assured a warm welcome at the Windsor. Every year she made an inspection trip to her claims until she was in her late eighties. At the age of 92 she insisted on flying over her properties to see them from the air.

As the years passed and mining disappeared, guests became fewer. But during the years of decline, Alice Jowett refused to lower her standards. Her spotless tablecloths and polished silver still greeted an occasional traveller. She typified a spirit of optimism which refused to let Trout Lake completely die. But in 1945 age forced her to sell the hotel after some 50 years. She remained in the Lardeau a few more years then entered a convalescent home at Kelowna. Here on November 5, 1953, she celebrated her birthday with a party and a cake bearing 100 candles. She died in 1955, going on for 102. Her ashes were returned to her beloved Lardeau and scattered among the mountains she loved.

The Windsor Hotel remained open to travellers, the bedrooms furnished with high square headboards belonging to the 1890s and carved dressers with mirrors which served guests at the turn of the century.

In the early 1980s there were new owners but by then the antique furnishings were gone. Modernized to conform to modern safety standards, the venerable Windsor is open from May to September to the general public then leased to skiers for the winter. Now nearing the century mark, it remains a link to the days when Trout Lake City was the jewel of the Lardeau. Mrs. Jowett would be proud.

Ferguson

Ferguson was located on a flat on Lardeau Creek about 4 miles (6.4 km) northeast of Trout Lake City. It was laid out in the early 1890s by the Ferguson brothers — Dave, Andrew, Peter and James — who owned the Triune Mine. As with similar communities stimulated by the prospect of rich mines and a railway, Ferguson grew fairly rapidly, despite its isolated location and mines so high that buildings were bolted to the mountainside and snow could fall every month.

By 1900 it listed five hotels among its business places, had electricity and a newspaper, the *Ferguson Eagle*. Its publisher, Richard Parmater Pettipiece, a name locals soon shortened to "Windy Parm," described Ferguson in glowing terms.

"It had," he wrote, "no banks, lawyers, highway robbers, policemen, smallpox or other infectious diseases. No cowbells, cats, engine bells, street-cars, public meetings, churches, theatres, blackjack dens, nickle-in-the-slot machines, or bush fires to keep one awake at night. In fact there is nothing to do but work, eat, read and sleep and enjoy the bright sunshine. Nearly 150 miners are at work in this neighborhood, blasting, picking and tearing out the precious ore...."

In the issue of December 12, 1901, he noted that Ferguson "is to have a brewery, a wholesale liquor store and another hotel; also a red light or two."

The 1903 edition of *The Year Book of British Columbia* reported that "Ferguson is the centre of the rich mining district of Trout Lake, commonly known as the Lardeau. A number of important shipping mines are tributary to this town. Among these are the Silver Cup, sold for $150,000 cash; the Nettie L. and the Triune, sold for $600,000. These are exceptionally rich in silver and lead. A branch line of railway from Kootenay Lake to Trout Lake, 35 miles in length, has recently been completed. This gives the district the necessary transportation facilities so long required. The population is about 400. Five hotels serve the public. A 30-ton vulcan smelter has been erected to treat local ores."

Unfortunately for the community, the smelter which was to treat local ores and "Mark a new era in the smelting and mining industry of B.C." cracked on its trial run. It was never used again. Other problems were the isolation and long winters with snow that could be 20 or more feet (6 m) deep. Ethel Garrett White was born in Ferguson in 1906 and spent her childhood in the community. She later recalled:

"We had a good skating rink in Ferguson. We used to skate a lot and my brothers were on the hockey team. My older brothers and sisters used to skate from Trout Lake to Gerrard over the lake. They used to get eight or nine feet of snow in Ferguson. It came in October and stayed until the last of May. In the winter we played on roof tops because the snow was right up even with the roof tops. There was no ploughing done. You just waded through it.

"We used to go by horse and buggy to Trout Lake. A tug went across to Gerrard then met the train. Or you could go out to Beaton and take a tug to Arrowhead and catch a train. In the winter it was terrible because

Trout Lake used to freeze over. They'd come over with a sleigh and buggy. A team of horses with a sleigh full of groceries went through the ice one time and they never did get them out."

Because of the isolation and virtual inaccessibility of the mines — the Wagner was at the 8,200-ft. (2,438-m) level — shipping costs were so high that only the best ore could be sent out for smelting. As the *Ferguson Eagle* once noted:

"It cost $25.20 to bring a car of feed from Calgary to Arrowhead over the C.P.R., a distance of over 300 miles in a mountainous section. It costs $42 to bring the same feed across the Arm from Arrowhead to Thompson's Landing, a distance of eleven miles." Even then the feed was still 16 miles (25 km) over a narrow dirt road from Ferguson.

The dirt road, however, was a highway compared with the access routes to many mines. Narrow trails switchbacked up the slopes to mines so high that even firewood had to be packed in on horses and mules. A name still associated with the packing is Andy Daney. Arriving in 1896 from Colorado where he had won a World Championship for packing with horses and mules, he remained in Ferguson for over 60 years — the life span of the community.

Since Andy guaranteed his work, his string of horses and mules was in steady demand, packing everything from eggs to a 600-pound cookstove. When an attempt was made to build an aerial tram from the lofty Triune Mine, Andy packed a cable up the switchback mountain trail. The cable was 1.5 miles (2.5 km) long and weighed several tons, but by tying his horses and mules head and tail in a line and distributing the weight over them all, he succeeded. Unfortunately, the aerial tramway was wrecked during the first winter.

Despite such disappointments, the community's residents remained confident of a prosperous future. In 1900 the *Ferguson Eagle* reflected on the general attitude when it reported that a ". . . matrimonial epidemic has struck this camp, evidently the direct outcome of increased prosperity in mining circles."

Among those involved in the "matrimonial epidemic" was Andy Daney. "FERGUSON'S POPULAR YOUNG PACKER GETS A LIFE CONTRACT," announced the paper. Then it stated: "At Trout Lake last Saturday, S. Daney of Ferguson and Miss Evelyn Jowett [daughter of Alice Jowett] were joined in matrimony. The *Eagle* joins their many friends in wishing them a happy and prosperous life."

The couple returned to Ferguson where Andy built a new house for his bride, complete with running water and electricity.

Unfortunately, Ferguson was not destined to survive. The price of metals dropped and the railway never arrived. The Nettie L, the Silver Cup and the other mines closed. Soon most buildings stood empty, although

Opposite page, top right: Andy Daney on his favorite horse, Steamboat, was synonymous with Ferguson. He lived there during the community's 60-year life span.

Opposite: Ferguson's decaying main street in the 1930s and, above it, the Lardeau Hotel in 1970. The last of Ferguson's five hotels, it has since disappeared, the victim of vandals and the region's heavy snowfall.

Andy Daney and his family remained in the community. In 1960 he and Evelyn celebrated their Diamond Wedding Anniversary, old-timers coming from all over the Lardeau to congratulate them.

Andy lived to be 93 but by then there was little left of the community he so loved. His son, Seldon, and his wife became the last permanent residents, continuing with the mail contract that Andy had held for half a century. But year by year the community disintegrated and finally of the five hotels only the Lardeau remained. Then it was gone, along with Andy Daney's house which was vandalized so badly that Seldon Daney burned it. The flames which curled upwards in the small bowl surrounded by snow-capped mountains were a Viking's pyre for the remains of a community that had been the hope of several hundred people.

Circle City and Ten Mile

Early promoters could never be accused of lacking vision. Their townsites, however remote, often appeared in literature as "cities" even though they were only lines on a surveyor's map. Typical was Circle City, some 12 miles (19 km) from Trout Lake City at the junction of Surprise Creek with the North Fork of Lardeau River. Its promoter was G.B. Batho of Ferguson. Envisioning it as terminus of a proposed railway, in the fall of 1901 he offered lots at $100 to $125. But there would be no railway — and within months no Circle City.

Vanishing with it was Ten Mile. Located at the junction of Gainer Creek and the South Fork of the Lardeau, it never exactly flourished. Ace Hillman ran a stopping place while a Ferguson merchant had a branch store. In the absence of a railroad, neither had any reason to remain. Ten Mile vanished.

Dawson City

Along the Lower Lardeau River rivals to Poplar appeared at the mouths of various creeks. Dawson City at Tenderfoot Creek was typical. It was optimistically christened by a man named Gilles who built a hotel. Angus MacDonald established a store and when the railroad crews arrived business thrived — but only briefly. For one summer it was a town of tents, and at Gilles' hotel three bartenders worked around the clock. But after the construction crews passed, Dawson City vanished.

Camborne

Born amid the nearly 10,000-ft (3,048-m) peaks of Glacier National Park, the Incomappleux River cuts its way southward to the Northeast Arm of Upper Arrow Lake. Silver-lead deposits were the first attraction, but in 1899 prospectors found a wide gold belt centered on Lexington Mountain. They staked and worked claims — the Spider, Beatrice and Silver Dollar — 7,000 ft. (2,133 m) up the mountainside, and the Eva at the mouth of Pool Creek. Further upriver were the rich Goldfinch and Oyster-Criterion. To supply them, a road was built 8 miles (12.8 km) from Beaton on Upper Arrow Lake, part of its route through the awesome Incomappleux River Canyon where timbers pinned it to vertical rock walls.

All of the activity inspired Cornish prospector Cory Menhinick to lay out the townsite of Camborne on flat land within a curve of the Incomappleux. In the summer of 1901 the Pendragon Hotel opened with a dance and to chronicle community events the *Camborne Miner* appeared, edited by clarinet-playing G.R. Northey. The town grew quickly, getting three stores, two halls, a Miners' Union, a brass band, and two stamp mills capable of turning out $12,000 gold bricks every month.

Camborne was geared to the fortunes of the mines. When winter snows buried mines buildings to the eaves, forcing shutdown; when forest fires burned tramway and bunkhouses; when reorganization changed owners and managers, Camborne suffered. When the mines finally failed, Camborne's shops and hotels gradually closed. In the fall of 1906 Northey published the last issue of the *Camborne Miner*.

But unlike most mining communities, there was a reprieve. In 1932

The above print from a damaged negative is a Mattie Gunterman photograph of local residents and the Coronation Hotel at Camborne in 1905.

Another of Mattie's photos shows the road from Beaton to Camborne. Here it is pinned to the rock walls of the Incompleux River.

Camborne flared briefly when the Meridian Mining Company consolidated several old properties. The outbreak of World War Two, however, ended activity. But there was to be another reprieve.

At war's end metal prices were high, resulting in several old claims on Lexington Mountain being reworked by Sunshine Lardeau Mines Limited. New machinery was installed in the old Meridian building and Camborne town rebuilt at the mouth of Pool Creek. Beginning in 1952, Sunshine Lardeau mined the steep hillside, crushing ore in the mill and shipping silver-lead-zinc concentrates to Cominco at Trail. Then came problems. In 1956 fire destroyed the plant at #10 portal, and later that spring the bunkhouse burned, killing one man. Sunshine Lardeau suspended operations May 14, 1958. This time there was no reprieve for Camborne City.

Goldfields

Beyond Camborne the rival townsite of Goldfields was laid out by Frank Goldsmith and Roger F. Perry, its purpose to supply the profitable Goldfinch Mine. A bridge was constructed across the Incomappleux River and Perry built a sawmill, the Pavilion Hotel, and became unofficial mayor. His hotel offered board from $2 up and boasted that "Rainier beer was always on hand, Hudson's Bay Company's best liquors were in stock and six-year-old whiskey on tap."

Perry strove to bring entertainment to the miners with one of the new "movie pictures" and even had a parade, but all was in vain. The Goldfinch Mine closed for lack of capital and Goldfields faded. The end was hastened in September 1906 when a cloudburst swept away the bridge, leaving an old trail from Comaplix the only access. As residents with their possessions struggled along it, they left behind their memories and another townsite to be engulfed by the forest.

The Lardeau was never to experience its dream of becoming a major mining region. Although appreciable gold values and important quantities of zinc were found, the complex ores were difficult to process. As a consequence, risk capital was hard to find. One by one the mines closed and communities vanished.

Today the mountainous Lardeau belongs to fishermen, campers, hikers, climbers and loggers. Its once flourishing communities live mainly in the yellowing pages of Colonel Lowery's and other newspapers, archival photos, government mine reports and the memories of an ever decreasing number of pioneers.

"The forest has almost repossessed the land," wrote backroads explorer Donovan Clemson, "though leaning headboards in smothered cemeteries still proclaim the names of long-dead miners and, occasionally, their wives and children. The devil's club and cow parsnip bury the rotting ruins of their homes. The unwary explorer stumbles over iron things: parts of machinery and old stoves, hidden in the ferns, and slips on old bottles concealed under the rich carpet of the moss — the ghostly relics of West Kootenay."

A selection of other HERITAGE HOUSE titles:

The PIONEER DAYS IN BRITISH COLUMBIA Series

Every article is true, many written or narrated by those who, 100 or more years ago, lived the experiences they relate. Each volume contains 160 pages in large format magazine size (8½ x 11), four-color covers, some 60,000 words of text and over 200 historical photos, many published for the first time.

A continuing Canadian best seller in three volumes which have sold over 75,000 copies. Each volume, $12.95

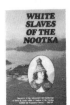

WHITE SLAVES OF THE NOOTKA

On March 22, 1803, while anchored in Nootka Sound on the West Coast of Vancouver Island, the *Boston* was attacked by "friendly" Nootka Indians. Twenty-five of her 27 crew were massacred, their heads "arranged in a line" for survivor John Jewitt to identify. Jewitt and another survivor became 2 of 50 slaves owned by Chief Maquina, never knowing what would come first ---- rescue or death.

The account of their ordeal, published in 1815, remains remarkably popular. New Western Canadian edition, well illustrated. 128 pages. $9.95

THE DEATH OF ALBERT JOHNSON: Mad Trapper of Rat River

Albert Johnson in 1932 triggered the greatest manhunt in Canada's Arctic history. In blizzards and numbing cold he was involved in four shoot-outs, killing one policeman and gravely wounding two other men before being shot to death.

This revised, enlarged edition includes photos taken by "Wop" May, the legendary bush pilot whose flying skill saved two lives during the manhunt. Another Canadian best seller. $7.95

OUTLAWS AND LAWMEN OF WESTERN CANADA

These true police cases prove that our history was anything but dull. Chapters in 160-page Volume Three, for instance, include Saskatchewan's Midnight Massacre, The Yukon's Christmas Day Assassins, When Guns Blazed at Banff, and Boone Helm — The Murdering Cannibal.

Each of the three volumes in this Canadian best seller series is well illustrated with maps and photos, with four-color photos on the covers. Volume One, $9.95; Volume Two, $8.95; Volume Three, $10.95

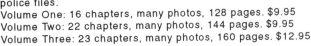

B.C. PROVINCIAL POLICE STORIES: Mystery and Murder from the Files of Western Canada's First Lawmen

The B.C. Police, born in 1858, were the first lawmen in Western Canada. During their 90 years of service they established a reputation as one of the most progressive police forces in North America. All cases in these best selling titles are reconstructed from archives and police files.

Volume One: 16 chapters, many photos, 128 pages. $9.95
Volume Two: 22 chapters, many photos, 144 pages. $9.95
Volume Three: 23 chapters, many photos, 160 pages. $12.95

B.C. BACKROADS

This best selling series contains complete information from Vancouver through the Fraser Canyon to Cache Creek, east to Kamloops country and north to the Cariboo. Also from Vancouver to Bridge River-Lillooet via Whistler. Each book contains mile-by-mile route mileage, history, fishing holes, wildlife, maps and photos.

Volume One — Garibaldi to Bridge River Country-Lillooet. $9.95
Volume Three — Junction Country: Boston Bar to Clinton. $9.95
Thompson-Cariboo: Highways, byways, backroads. $4.95

An Explorer's Guide: MARINE PARKS OF B.C.

To tens of thousands of boaters, B.C.'s Marine Parks are as welcome and convenient as their popular highway equivalents. This guide includes anchorages and onshore facilities, trails, picnic areas, campsites, history and other information. In addition, it is profusely illustrated with color and black and white photos, maps and charts.

Informative reading for boat owners from runabouts to cabin cruisers. 200 pages $12.95.

GO FISHING WITH THESE BEST SELLING TITLES

HOW TO CATCH SALMON — BASIC FUNDAMENTALS

The most popular salmon book ever written. Information on trolling, rigging tackle, most productive lures, proper depths, salmon habits, downriggers, where to find fish, and much more.

Sales over 130,000. 176 pages. $5.95

HOW TO CATCH SALMON — ADVANCED TECHNIQUES

The most comprehensive advanced salmon fishing book available. Over 200 pages crammed full of how-to-tips and easy-to-follow diagrams. Covers all popular salmon fishing methods: mooching, trolling with bait, spoons and plugs, catching giant chinook, and a creel full of other information.

A continuing best seller. 192 pages. $11.95

HOW TO CATCH CRABS: How popular is this book? This is the 11th printing, with sales over 90,000. $4.95

HOW TO CATCH BOTTOMFISH: Revised and expanded. $5.95

HOW TO CATCH SHELLFISH: Updated 4th printing. 144 pages. $3.95

HOW TO CATCH TROUT by Lee Straight, one of Canada's top outdoorsmen. 144 pages. $5.95

HOW TO COOK YOUR CATCH: Cooking seafood on the boat, in a camper or at the cabin. 8th printing. 192 pages. $4.95

FLY FISH THE TROUT LAKES

with Jack Shaw

Professional outdoor writers describe the author as a man "who can come away regularly with a string when everyone else has been skunked." In this book, he shares over 40 years of studying, raising and photographing all forms of lake insects and the behaviour of fish to them.

Written in an easy-to-follow style. 96 pages. $8.95

SALMON FISHING BRITISH COLUMBIA: Volumes One and Two Since B.C. has some 7,000 miles of coastline, a problem to its 400,000 salmon anglers is where to fish. These books offer a solution. Volume One includes over 100 popular fishing holes around Vancouver Island. Volume Two covers the Mainland Coast from Vancouver to Jervis Inlet. Both include maps, gear to use, best times, lures and a tackle box full of other information.

Volume One — Vancouver Island. $9.95
Volume Two — Mainland Coast: Vancouver to Jervis Inlet. $11.95

Heritage House books are sold throughout Western Canada. If not available at your bookstore you may order direct from Heritage House, Unit 8, 17921 55 Ave., Surrey, B.C. V3S 6C4. Payment can be by cheque or money order but please add $1.00 a book to help pay postage and handling.